NICOLE C

# FROM STRIVING TO THRIVING

## NOT ONLY SURVIVING

GOD IS AMAZING AND SO ARE YOU

KNOWING WHO YOU ARE
AND
BEING WHO HE CREATED YOU TO BE

Trilogy Christian Publishers
A Wholly Owned Subsidiary of Trinity Broadcasting Network
2442 Michelle Drive
Tustin, CA 92780

10 9 8 7 6 5 4 3 2 1
Library of Congress Cataloging-in-Publication Data is available.
ISBN 979-8-89041-422-9

ISBN (ebook) 979-8-89041-423-6

# Dedication

In memory of
my wonderful grandmother "Nenu" Velma Faye Purswell
Matthews (2-3-1923)
and
father Don Stanley Coleman (11-28-1948)

# Introduction with Words of Wisdom

"In the beginning was the Word, and the Word was with God and the Word was God." John 1:1 NKJV.
We are eternal along with God. Romans 6:23 NLT says, "For the wages of sin is death, but the free gift of God is eternal life in Christ Jesus our Lord."
"All scripture is God-breathed and is useful for teaching, rebuking, correcting and
training in righteousness (2 Timothy 3:16, NIV).
In today's world, we need to be mindful of everyone. We should not offend or allow intentional offending by others. People should not be allowed to use what was meant in the past to bring justice and equality to separate and divide more by being divisive to control and oppress others.
Romans 14:16, NIV says, "Therefore do not let what you know is good be spoken of as 1 evil."
The devil is the accuser of the brethren - rebuke that.
We are to LOVE and pray for offenders and the offended without passing judgement on either.
Speak positive affirmations. Just like eating fruits and vegetables brings life, declare God's Word (Life) over yourself and your family daily.
God's word is practical wisdom.
Just because something happens doesn't mean that we must go along with it or that's how it is meant to be. We must discern God's direction and we may need to fight against it or say no.
No weapon formed against us shall prosper.
Controller/patriarch-relationship. In fact, some parts of the body that seem weakest and least important are actually the most necessary (1 Corinthians 12:22)

You are blessed.
Be what He called you to be.
Get up. The KEY is to keep on going and don't give up (you can't fail). What might seem like failure could be a step back in order to find something better or to elevate to the next level.
You already have everything that you need; now go get what you want!

# Table of Contents

# FROM STRIVING TO THRIVING

# Chapter One
# My Life

I am an overcomer. I was raised in Southeast Texas. My parents divorced when I was five years old. I have a sister who is four years older than me. I lived with my mom until the age of 12. Prior to moving in with my grandmother, my weekends alternated between my father's house and my maternal grandmother's house. I spent every summer at my grandma's. My days at home were mostly spent alone playing with Barbies, video games, or watching TV. I rode bikes on the greenbelt trail. It felt more like home at my grandmother's. I swam and she was usually there. She cooked and watched TV with me. We would sometimes read the Bible and she tickled my back at night and allowed me to sleep with her often. I remember crying hard, looking out the rear window most of the way home on Sunday nights.

One of my favorite people growing up was my only sister. Little did I know then that she was my worst enemy. I wanted to be just like her! She talked about herself as if she were the greatest thing on earth and led me to believe that I was inferior. Needless to say, that relationship turned out devasting and null. My sister said that I annoyed her and would emotionally (verbally) and physically push me away. She called me fat and stupid, pulled my hair, and hit me for years. One day she even sat on me naked, held my arms down above my head and moved her body up and sat on my face. I was in fourth grade. The same year she locked me out of the house and I ended up breaking a window to get back in. When I tried to lock her outside, she cut off the breaker box in the garage. She called me names, ridiculed my prepubescent body parts, and said that I should be a model for Lane Bryant. She would do things such as convince me to give her my allowance and get me to do things such as tickle her back but never reciprocate. My grandmother told me when I got big enough to take up for myself that my sister would stop being physically violent. Boy, was she right. Not only did the violence stop, my sister went on to end the relationship after my dad signed his will over to her. Then she froze me out of caring for him.

My mother was gone most evenings, working in sales and trying to provide a better life for us. She got involved in a cult (Ramtha) and moved to Washington State for about a year. I went with her for two weeks and flew back to move in with my grandmother. My mom's dad was an elder in the Church of Christ. My dad's father was mayor pro tem in Shepherd, Texas. I also had a great cousin who was the Justice of the Peace of the town which I called home and a second cousin who was mayor pro tem there.

Well, back to the story of my sister. When I was 15 years old, and she was married, I stood up for myself and hit her back. She put me out of the car. I received an apology letter from her for all the years of abuse shortly after, and the physical aspect never happened again. My kids and I often visited her as I was working as a medical assistant with two small children. She would convince me to pay for half of Mom's and Dad's expensive Christmas gifts even though her husband made $100,000 per year and I was making less than $20,000, single and had two small kids to buy for. She also would have me contribute to Christmas dinner and years later I found out that Dad was sending her money to pay for it and never once did she mention that or offer to reimburse me. She was always trying to make me feel as if I was less than or that something was wrong with me. The controlling behavior is still happening today. One Christmas at her house she and my father told me that she would be in charge of all of his end-of-life arrangement and that she was to be in charge of halving all of his assets with me. She took me to court and testified against me with CPS trying to adopt my two older children. We never had a relationship after this. Did my parents not recognize that she ended our relationship right after my dad changed his will, "to protect it from getting stolen from me by my husband to only have it stolen from me by her"? I spoke to him years later at his house and he told me that he would add me back in his will since it had been years and I had not returned to my ex. I was in Nurse Practitioner school. I called his attorney and told them from his house and the attorney's wife told me that I had to bring him there and then she asked me if I knew how to do taxes because they had been asking my sister for them. At that time I did not not know how and I got confused and scared. I called my sister on the way home and notified her. I asked her if she would pay me with his money to keep taking off of work and driving that far to help take care of him. I didn't hear from her again. She moved in with him and sold his house. His friend told me that I should get half. I got nothing.

I spoke with her in 2018 regarding this and she stated that she didn't remember that. She did, however, say that there was a small life insurance policy in my name. She has sold his house and her house and is living in the house that he purchased, has control of all his accounts (she has him in a memory care unit) and has distributed his vehicles to herself and her sons. She offered to help me pay for two $700 classes and then asked when I would be paying her back.

During that time, I was on welfare and raising three younger kids (ten, nine, and five) with my 18-year-old living in my garage. My 20-year-old is living in a dorm at college. As far as I know, no one else in my family has had to apply for welfare. My aunt was a huge part of my support system until they all went against me in court with CPS. I had been completely sober from 2-26-2008 until 2016 when I relapsed. They have never been sober. Yet even during that time I still was not good enough for them. I believe that my mom does not drink or take any pills (anxiety/pain) but the rest of my family members (sister, brother-in-law, nephews, aunt, cousin and her daughter) do. It took years for my mom to even talk to me, much less believe a word that I said. She always listened to and believed my sister. My cousin and her daughter spoke against me to their mom. I loved her and believed that she loved me growing up. She did tell me that I annoyed her, and she called me "Nik the Tick." She cared for me and was there for me after my grandmother died. Despite these individuals' own faults, they tried to manipulate like I was the bad one, oppressed me. Some have said that they tried to make themselves feel better by thinking they were better than me. I believe that we should all be winners as we are all from the same family and shouldn't compete but lift each other up and help each other to thrive. It is hard enough out in the world. But God. He has sent me numerous Christian brothers and sisters to help me overcome the many obstacles in my life. In scripture Proverbs 18:24 refers to Jesus as a friend that sticks closer than a brother. God has taught me that I can ALWAYS depend on Him and not look to my own family. He is my provider, my protector, my healer, and my redeemer.

Provider: Philippians 4:19 (ESV) says, "And my God will supply every need of yours according to his riches in glory in Christ Jesus." The key here is that He owns everything; ask big! Expect big! In Matthew 7:11 (NIV) it states, "If you then,

who are evil, know how to give good gifts to your children, how much more will your Father who is heaven give good things to those who ask him!" Psalms 34:10 says that those who seek the Lord shall not lack ANY good thing.
Healer: Psalm 103:2 (ESV) says, "Bless the Lord, Oh my soul, and forget not all His benefits, who forgives all your iniquity, who heals all your diseases, who redeems your life from the pit, who crowns you with steadfast love and mercy, who satisfies you with good so that your youth is renewed like the eagle's…" Also, in James 5:14 it says that if anyone is sick to have the elders pray over them and anoint them with oil in the name of the Lord.

Redeemer: 2 Corinthians 9:8 (ESV), "And God is able to make all grace abound to you, so that having all sufficiency in all things at all times, you may abound in every good work." In John 5:24 (ESV) Jesus says, "Truly, truly, I say to you, whoever hears my word and believes him who sent me has eternal life. He does not come into judgment, but passes from death to life."

These same family members that kept me away from my husband acting like it was different than what goes on in other lives also were abused. Growing up I saw my aunt hit by her drunk, cheating husband. She stayed. Her granddaughter has been hit by her husband, and she has stayed. She went to CPS against me and my ex as stated prior. No one has called CPS on her but just the opposite; they help her with the kids. I loved her so much as an infant and child. I'm not sure why she grew up to hate me. While sitting in court she raised her hand to show me that she was wearing my expensive ring that my grandmother left for me. I had sold it to her mom before I went through bankruptcy to try and save my house (at her suggestion). Years later my cousin went to a CPS meeting and was against me again telling them bad things about me with her mother. I had asked my aunt to go to court and testify for my daughters who cried out to her about the sexual abuse by their father, but my niece yelled at me saying that I was crazy. That she needed her to babysit her boy that day even though her husband's mom didn't work, and loved to babysit him. My aunt wrote a note about the incident that she observed. My niece invited me over one day. She had a Band Aid over my face in our family portrait. She told me that I couldn't be a nurse but should be a respiratory therapist. (This is where we must be careful about the advice that we listen to, and this goes back to "friends" destroying each other.) I did make it through nursing school and passed the board exam on my first try with God's help. God made that possible with my aunt's (when our relationship was somewhat restored after CPS court until the passing of her husband when she moved in with her daughter) help babysitting in the evenings so that I could go to school two evenings a week while working fulltime.

My father was an alcoholic in the Army before I was born. He was married three times, a womanizer, a businessman and very outgoing with friends. Also, he was very stern and conservative. He took me to many places as a child. My mom did not, except when she moved (Washington/Oklahoma) and then when I was older and my two older kids were smaller, we went to Florida to Universal Studios and Disney World. My dad took us to Galveston (beach), New Braunfels (the river), San Antonio (the River Walk), Astroworld (theme park), and out to eat a lot. He also took us ice skating, to ride go karts, and horses.

When with my mom's mom we attended church regularly. My grandfather passed away the year prior to my moving in. As a child I looked to food as an escape. (I think I still do sometimes). I have to fight (pray and fast) against that. As I got older in my teens, I turned to tobacco, drugs, and alcohol. My sister had moved out on her own at the same time that I moved in with my grandmother. I stopped going to my dad's. I started smoking cigarettes and then marijuana. After being threatened by several girls with tennis rackets in gym my first week of high school, I went to multiple schools in the area (including three private schools). I tried basketball and cheer. I never felt like I belonged. I would make a poor choice, feel guilty and then self-sabotage (hang with bad influences) or give up and stop pursuing anything positive as I couldn't see the forest for the trees. At 15 years old I was taken to Cornerstone Church by a friend that I stayed with often. I fell in love with Jesus and was baptized. I learned about suddenlies (receiving devine intervention immediately) and how I am a priest (Child of God). "And you will be called priests of the Lord, you will be named ministers of our God. You will feed on the wealth of nations and in their riches you will boast." (Isaiah 61:6, NIV)

I got to experience nuclear families. It didn't stick at that time. I was still smoking and couldn't stop (didn't think that I could). So, I thought that I wasn't worthy. I went out looking for men/boys to love me. In public school I was led astray. I was able to skip, smoke, and do drugs on campus. I thought that no one knew. God knew! My senior year, I had skipped too many days to graduate. So, I took my GED and moved to the country town my dad was living in (owning and running a BBQ restaurant after years of professional sales in Houston with his third wife) and started junior college. I got an apartment, went to school full-time and tried working at four different places: Casa Ole, Country Bakery, a grocery store, and the Washington County Chamber of Commerce.

My biology teacher was teaching Darwinism as a fact; boy did that confuse me. An old boyfriend on crack stole my rent money from my glove compartment. Instead of confessing to my dad and asking for help, I moved back into my grandmother's.

At age 18 I went to jail for possession of marijuana. I went to rehab and was put on probation. I started attending AA meetings. I stopped smoking marijuana after failing a urinalysis on probation, going to jail for a weekend, and them extending it. Then I started drinking alcohol because "it is legal." I also tried other drugs here and there but was too scared to get addicted as I liked my material possessions. I was extremely promiscuous and even raped on several occasions.

When I was 20 my dad took me to rehab in South Houston then to Santa Maria from San Jacinto County Jail after being in a car with some guys that were arrested for committed aggravated robbery of a drug dealer. I became pregnant with my daughter. I found out during that trial and thankfully it got dismissed.

I became pregnant with my daughter at age 20. I found out while in the middle of that case that got dismissed. I remember praying and asking for forgiveness in court and asking God for the opportunity to raise her to follow Him. My grandmother had asked me to leave her house (if I wanted to continue my partying lifestyle) when I was pregnant with Paige. I moved to a government apartment. I worked at Pizza Hut. My apartment got robbed by a boy that I was "dating." I started Medical Assistant school.

I then got pregnant when my daughter was only 11 months

old. I told my parents that I was pregnant finally, after five or six months; I was so scared and nauseous. My mom and I had gone to dinner at Landry's in Galveston and were staying at the Flagship with the baby. They took me to San Antonio to have an abortion. I did the paperwork and was in the waiting room. My mom, dad and daughter were outside. I heard a voice in my head that said, "What if this is your boy?" My mom came in and said, "It's never too late until it's too late." I told her that I did not want to do it. By the grace of God, I walked out and didn't go through with it. That man (my son) literally just walked through my room as I'm typing this. He graduated high school a month and a half ago. He is currently not serving God, but I know that he will. Proverbs 22:6 KJV "Train up a child in the way he should go: and when he is old, he will not depart from it." I have also had several words spoken over him that he will be a pastor someday.

My dad didn't speak to me for a couple of years. I completed medical assistant school even though my dad had told me to attend certified nurse's aide school. I moved several years after into my mother's lake cabin. I was still drinking and "dating." I was attending the Church of Christ sporadically with my two small children. When they were two and three years old, I tried to commit suicide. I was feeling hopeless. My thoughts were that I would never be able to quit drinking or have a husband. The house was far from town and there were some plumbing issues as well. I was working as a sales rep for my dad's medical supply company. It was mostly alone from home but involved some traveling marketing to nursing homes. I was in ICU for three days and then we moved in with my mom. I stayed sober for 30 days, attending AA. I started working back in a doctor's office. We moved to my grandmother's house for a while. The kids and I moved to an apartment. I was then able to buy my first home. I was going to work every day; I started drinking and sleeping around again. My grandmother was still helping me with the kids. She took them to school and church. My oldest daughter stayed with her a lot. My grandmother then started to get dementia.

I then met my soon-to-be husband when the kids were five and six. I moved in with him three months after we met. I thought that I could continue drinking. We argued a lot. We were physically and verbally abusive to each other. I left him. He destroyed my nice furniture, got rid of all my clothes, spray painted TVs, flattened tires, broke radiators and cut cords to appliances. We got back together. We moved back into my house. He was abusing me and calling the cops on me (when I would try to leave); he would lie and put the blame on me. I went to jail several times. He flipped me off once as I was in a police car after I tried to flee with kids barefoot and he yelled out for me to come back for my purse and keys. Another time, he planted a gun in the front yard and told the police that I was in some way using it. I had never even touched the gun. He finally went to jail three months after we were married. He had punched me and my five-year-old son directly in the face. My thought at the time: I would never be with a man that hit my kid. I had that bruise with a knot on my face for three weeks. I filed for divorce. The DA called me a year later to prosecute. I thought that he was out of our lives for good. I didn't realize at the time that he was saying for sure that he would prosecute. I let fear of going to court influence me to decline I didn't understand how that would significantly affect the rest of our lives and him getting away with hurting me and the children more.

I went to Santa Maria (rehab) again in 2007, where God told me during a service at Mercy Street and through His word that I would get my children back. "I will say to the north and south, 'Bring my sons and daughters back to Israel from the distant corners of the earth. Bring all who claim me as their God, for I have made them for my glory. It was I who created them." Isaiah 43: 6-7 (NLT).

I was living back with my grandmother and her dementia was progressing. I was still drinking. I went back to him. My family made me move out of her house. I wasn't partying or dating multiple men. I had been past that for quite some time. I was able to take care of Nenu but my family did not allow me to. I have seen other families too where they have pushed out the one that loved the person that needed caretaking. I loved her and was more than able to at that time. They ended up letting my aunt move in to caretake and eventually sending Nenu to a nursing home.

We tried marriage counseling with the preacher from the Church of Christ. CPS was now involved. We separated several more times. I was all the while trying to quit drinking. I was ordered to attend intensive outpatient. I slowed down and tried to hide my drinking. My children were taken away. I thought it was his fault. He was gone. He left the night that CPS took the kids. I got notice of the house being foreclosed on. I contemplated suicide. I was lying down on the railroad tracks directly in front of my house for what seemed to be forever. Although, I had learned with previous attempt that it doesn't help anything to progress but sets your life back further. Example: I was making good money in a stable home with my kids but felt helpless because of the drinking and loneliness; when in reality it wasn't as bad as I thought, and I probably could have just moved to a different location. By trying to commit suicide it took me backwards into my mom's house and caused the loss of a good-paid job. Not to mention the diagnosis of depression from the history of suicide attempt just recently even though it was over 20 years ago. So, I went home to my house that was to be foreclosed on. I was crying in the carport when two men that attend Cornerstone showed up. I know it was God. Everything was pretty much a blur, but God stepped in. We moved in with my husband's brother and his sister-in-law, who were never truly friendly to me despite my efforts. We got a rental house with the help of Cornerstone, and he was working. I missed my kids so badly, sometimes the pain felt as if they were dead. I cried daily. CPS told me that I had to leave him and go to rehab even though I had stopped drinking at this point. My husband got violent again on top of me in kitchen, hit and choked me. That's when I realized that it wasn't my drinking that caused him to be abusive like he had been saying. I went to a neighbor's and an elder from the church picked me up. I lost memorable things that were very important to me (grandmother's keepsakes, kid's Christmas ornaments and my two oldest's baby books). My (God-serving) second cousin let me stay at her house and I read A Purpose Driven Life by Rick Warren. This book is an eye-opening life changer which helps our thought processes and makes life easier to live by giving hope and instilling knowledge that we are not alone in our thought processes. There are others who think the same way and that we do have a purpose to do God's will and bring others into His Kingdom to better their lives.

I went to a couple of women's shelters and then to Teen Challenge. In Teen Challenge we read a chapter of Proverbs every morning and for the first 30 days were immersed completely in the Bible, specifically the gospels, and writing a summary for each chapter while memorizing verses during the day. We attended other Bible studies and church at night. This is also life changing (getting the Word of God in you progresses your physical self forward into the purpose that God has for you). It took losing my kids for God to open up my eyes and let Him in to heal me from my past. He made me the mom that I had always prayed to be. His promises are true. His will is to bless us and give us the desires of our hearts. My husband also went to Teen Challenge. I had hopes of the kids eventually coming to live there but my mom wouldn't even let them visit. While in Teen Challenge, they took me to a local hospital as I was having severe "labor pains." I had an ectopic pregnancy and thus a miscarriage. They allowed my husband to go with me to the hospital and stay.

He left me at Teen Challenge and went home to his parents. I left after him and went to him. We were now living at his parents' house who did not serve God. Not long after, he was abusive again. I left and went to a women's shelter. Then my mom picked me up and sent me on a bus back to Teen Challenge. I then left Teen Challenge again and rode the bus back to Houston, although the word that I had put in me there was still in my heart and working in my life.

We lived with his parents for a while; I was very depressed. I cried when cartoons would even pass on the TV Guide. I remember thinking how sick of cartoons that I had gotten from watching then for years with my children. At that point I realized how much I preferred to be with them and watch cartoons than watch anything else without them. My mom allowed us to move into her lake house. My mom was still fostering my children per CPS. I got pregnant with my middle daughter. My husband got physically violent with me. I was still sober from 2-26-2008. I moved into the ministry house. I was still visiting the kids and doing everything CPS was telling me to do. I had stopped drinking since 2-26-2008. I got a job at a doctor's office in my hometown while volunteering at the church. This is when CPS (with my sister) took me to court to terminate my rights in Liberty County. My sister was trying to adopt them, against me, stating that I was unfit. Ladies from the church went with me and helped me believe that I could get them back. I cried daily for those few years and sometimes I believed the lies of the enemy, such as I would never get my kids back. The children's attorney ad litem had an awesome closing argument despite how I thought she felt toward me during the entire process. It had to be the Holy Spirit speaking through her. My rights were not terminated by a jury!

My ex-husband came to the ministry house one night and I called the police, but he hid in the woods and later told me that he watched them. He started back to church. Hurricane Ike came and I moved in with him, into an apartment across the street from my mother's condo where my other two children were; I was very pregnant with our first child. I had her a couple of months after (on his birthday). A week after she was born, I was in the bath getting ready for us to take her to her first newborn follow-up appointment. He said that he was running to McDonald's to get breakfast and never came back. He had taken my baby. I was breastfeeding. He said that I wasn't. I went across the street to my mom's and pumped. Her townhome and my older children were directly across the street. I cried a lot and felt as if I had lost a limb. I screamed out to God and worshipped Him, listening to "Return from Egypt" by Pastor Del Mar. I quit smoking again which I had restarted during the hurricane. I filed for divorce again.

I got my baby back a week later. There was a Texas State Trooper that lived in the complex. I notified him that my estranged husband was bringing the baby back and told him when because I was scared how he would react or if he would hurt us or not leave. He did leave but when he left, he filed false charges on me. I stayed with a mentor from Cornerstone for a while. I found out that I had a warrant for his false charges. He stated that I got the baby back at a motel in next town and that I had poked his eye and snatched her from her car seat by her arm. They had felony charges against me. It took a while for them to be dropped. I prayed and trusted in the Lord. I called a shelter but was able to stay at my mentor's house until court. My attorney told me to turn myself in but instead I contacted the agency and gave them the contact information of the state trooper who had witnessed the truth. I had to meet with a detective and give a statement. Went to court in Harris County. I told an account of my husband abusing me in Dallas, on his job training trip, where there were several witnesses. I remember lying under the toilet, after being pushed down and hitting it, unable to move from him and screaming for help. His attorney asked what I would say if he said that the people from Dallas were outside and that helped my case more than my own attorney did. I got to stay in the apartment with Bree. Cornerstone helped pay rent for a month or two. They got me a car and I got a job in the Medical Center in Houston. I was working full-time, going to counseling once a week, domestic violence class, parenting for the third time, AA and continuing to go to church two or three times per week. I started volunteering in the nursery. The judge in Harris County ordered several classes. I completed the Aid to Victims of Domestic Abuse (AVDA) program. He started the Battering Intervention and Prevention (BIPP) program but didn't finish it. I paid for my half of the home study; he did not. The judge ruled on my behalf in the best interests of the baby.

I met up with my ex-husband on Valentine's Day. I got pregnant with our second child. CPS told me that I would never get my older children back. I did not give up. I continued going to classes and doing everything that I was supposed to according to CPS's plan. I was reading my Bible daily and praying. God moved. One of the pastors/elders couples kept me encouraged often during prayer meetings. I remember him saying, "You've come a long way, baby," and her saying, "BUT GOD," referring to things which seemed impossible like the judge telling me that I wouldn't get my children back to raise them according to the Word in the admonition of the Lord, in church and train them up the way that they should go.

My baby and I moved to an apartment in Cleveland. My grandmother passed away about this time; she was transitioned from the nursing home to an LTAC. I was working at the doctor's office in Houston. My older kids had a stair step progression and moved back in with me. I had the baby. This was 2009. My ex-husband came back and we got engaged. We didn't have sex for those eight months. Three weeks before the wedding we slept together for a few days. I knew it was wrong so I stopped. He left again. I had two miscarriages and I made it through with God (one I got very sick with a high temperature). I didn't tell anyone and even went to work the same day, except I confessed to my prayer intercessor mentor.

One night his brother poured a whole bottle of anointing oil on his head at one of the many prayer meetings that we attended. The pastor spoke to him that his life would be destroyed if he didn't change. We separated for several years. I remained faithful to God in church.

During that time, I learned to hear the voice of God. I heard that my oldest daughter would make the cheerleading team, I heard that I was going to have another boy, and I heard that I was going to make it into nursing school.

I volunteered a lot: One Day with God- prison ministry, I was on the Miriam's dance team for a couple of years, I worked in the nursery for four years, participated in multiple outreaches such as school supplies charities and hallelujah nights, feeding the elderly and was part of the transitional prayer team.
We remarried in 2012 after dating for four months. We separated two months later due to him having an affair with his manager. I got pregnant with our third child three weeks prior to the divorce. I tested positive three days after. We had gone to counseling but he was still lying to and trying to look good for the counselor instead of working on our relationship. I later found out that men use the counselor to promote themselves for court instead of to work on issues within themselves or fix relationship problems.

During nursing school, I had my last baby. Another boy. That was my final divorce. He cheated on me with my old apartment landlord where he was working maintenance. After I found out that he had molested my two daughters. I never returned to him again. It takes what it takes, and I guess that is what it took. I never thought that would happen, but I always told myself that I would believe my children if they ever told me. The judge didn't believe me when I stood up for my children and allowed for supervised visits at his mom's where it continued the next year. The girls went through several forensic interviews. Their therapist took evidence to the Montogomery County Grand Jury but they didn't indite him. After that he had multiple opportunities for stairstep visits in public places that he never completed. Thankfully, God has kept them protected.

I started working six 12 hour shifts per week. I progressed and was promoted at work. I stopped going to AA thinking, that I was getting recovery at work. I also felt that AA was more toward the dark side than church. While they believed in God and tried to spread the message, they did not proclaim freedom but to be forever chained in the past and character defects, or at least this is what my future boyfriend would teach in the AA group that he led.

I started dating. I dated one man from church. I had the cops come remove him from my house after he threw a remote at my head and it stuck in the wall. He was also gone on the weekends (I think doing drugs and dating others). I started drinking again in 2016. The next guy that I dated I believed that we had fallen in love, but his baby momma was using me as a come up or as an opportunity to advance herself. They stole a vehicle from me and threatened me multiple times. I started dating an old boyfriend that was released from prison. He helped me get the truck back and I thought that he was protecting me from them as they would drive by and threaten to burn my house down. There were weapons in my truck when I got it back. I don't know why she continued to threaten me after she had him back. That guy started selling drugs again and I started dating a police officer who helped protect me from him as he became violent, and his baby momma beat me up severely. I received two DWI's in one week. I got fired.

My mother and sister made me go back to Santa Maria Hostel for 30 days after leaving me in jail for 11. I had to notify the Texas Board of Nursing. I was placed on TPAPN (Texas Peer Assistance Program for Nurses). I had to check in daily and do random drug tests for years. They made it more and more difficult for me to work, even though I never had a drug diversion. I am still sober since the last DWI in April of 2017. While at Mercy Street Church I believed that God told me one of the leaders was to be my husband – I heard him sing LOVE, I heard him say we will be married in group, I remember his name from an altar call at Cornerstone and his last initial from a glimpse when I worked at a video/pizza store as a teenager. I dated him for 1½ years. I sold my house and lost my job after changing jobs to move in with him. I had been sober but went to work after an episode of domestic violence where I was physically impaired and emotionally unstable to perform and communicate properly at work (The HCA StaRN Program).

He looked like the cop that I had been dating. The cop had carried my purse into Liberty County jail when I was transported after getting my DWI. He said, "It is over." He acted just like my first husband. I thought he was him in another body. At times I believe it was the devil. I fooled myself into believing that was all that I deserved. I had read worldly stuff that said that my partner was a mirror of me. I know today that I have not done the stuff that they have. I have never molested a child or continued to oppress people just to take their money. People should receive Jesus and then have freedom to elevate, not be told that they are crazy or that their past will always be who they are and that they should look at the negative of themselves every day. We are to know who we are in Christ. We are loved. We are redeemed.

I stayed with him when off work- he watched the kids while I was at work. I would cry every time that I left him. I read an email from his ex that said that all she does is cry every day. I also read an email from him to her saying "I care for you, I'm just not ready." I read one that said "Call me" even though he told me that her number was always blocked and that he never talked to her. I read that she was having an STD test done. He stated that he never wanted to talk to her and didn't want her emailing him. She sent an email while out of state that said "I'm scared that you are getting back with Nicole." We were on a trip out of town together and I saw him emailing her then. He stated that he had gone through the same thing with her about me even though he told me that he never tried to get back together with her. I had also seen his messages on a dating website where he called many women beautiful and stunning. He spoke about meeting up with them. On the night before his grandson was born, he was texting me yet messaging some other woman as well and she accused him of talking to someone else and he said that he wasn't. That same night he texted me angrily about accusing him about talking to other women, but I wasn't.

He said that I was his wife, and we would be back together. He said that he had financial stuff to work out. He blamed me for not paying bills. He took the money that I had given him for a car note. He said that child support was taken out of his account, therefore he allocated my car note money to that. I used to wonder why he left instead of marrying me. I was walking and praising, reading the Bible daily, and fasting. I truly believed that he was supposed to be my husband and I still have these thoughts daily that rage war in my head. I then remember that he was racist saying blacks have a harder life even though I had given him multiple examples of my life being hard. I was beaten up by a Hispanic female officer prior to incarceration after having my life threatened and going to them for help. He used people's losses for monetary gain, he directs them in a way to keep them down rather than building them up and giving them the tools and knowledge to grow, prosper and  better their lives. He chose to leave rather than marry me. I do know that it was God's plan but he did not submit to God, so I had to move on and not hang on to that hope and ruin the rest of my life. My heart was broken, and I felt loss every day when I awoke despite all the violence that had occurred. He had other beliefs that I did not agree with such as: the world is flat, he called me a low life B, he beat me up multiple times and never apologized but blamed me. He is a Democrat (not that it is bad but the type of Democrat that puts Republicans down and promotes evil as good). He talked about Trump and others being sexual with others as if we all haven't been. He told me that I acted like a victim and a fake Christian. He listened to worldly music and watched shows that made me feel uncomfortable, but I was willing to look past all of that because I believed that he was to be my husband. Also that everybody has issues and is not perfect but he was not willing to look past my flaws. In fact, he played the victim and maybe I believed at times that he was/is a fake Christian or that he just has a pornography problem which goes into his physical problem of wanting to and being with others physically. The counselor at Lakewood told me to investigate his email. I saw emails, Facebook messages, and multiple dating site accounts even though he told me that he wanted to be alone. I saw an email saying that he had finally left me and that he wanted to see her. He asked for a picture of her butt "again." She said that she was lying beside her boyfriend. He asked one woman to marry him on Valentine's Day through a Facebook message. His ex from two years ago was constantly messaging him and he told her that he cared about her, but he wasn't ready, and she said that she would wait. He was even messaging her when we went out of town for my birthday three months after our separation. He told one lady that he wasn't talking to anyone else one night and I figured it out to be one night when he was talking to me telling me that his grandson would be born the next day. He had also gotten upset with me that night when I asked him the same thing, yet he went off on me and blamed me, saying that my jealousy was the reason we didn't get along. He texted me the day of my dad's memorial and unfriended me on Facebook and asked me for $12,000 the next day.

I continued down the rabbit hole with TPAPN. They sent me to three psych evaluations despite me sending them records from the one just taken when rehab sent me to Harris County Mental Health and I was diagnosed with adjustment disorder. The first two diagnosed me with anxiety. So, after being fired they sent me for an even more invasive neuro-psych eval. After the second psych eval I was told to start volunteering again. I served on the Sanctuary Medical Alert team at Lakewood in Houston. I was then discharged from TPAPN and placed back with the Board of Nursing. I had to take an assessment class in person and then complete the K-Star program. My license was never revoked but during that time was placed on disciplinary status with stipulations. The stipulations were the classes. My RN license was restored (unencumbered) just prior to graduating from Nurse Practitioner school which they were aware of.

God is mighty. He can restore anything. Our destiny will be fulfilled despite our own actions or the actions of others trying to hinder it. Keep hope. Pray, praise, and speak God's Word. Declare His promises back to Him on your life. Trust God in everything. Pray for His will to be done; it is the best for everyone no matter what we think. We will be taken care of and provided for but should not let others oppress us and use us. It is great to serve and there is persecution, but we are made to be the head and above.

We have purpose. We have joy when we are walking in His purpose and in His divine plan. He is our Provider. He will not only bring what we need but will give us wealth when we tithe. Health: He is the healer and will restore health. He will bless us to be a blessing. He gives us favor with Him and with others. I used to not understand why things in my life didn't seem stable. I would see it in others' lives (marriages, jobs for long periods); sometimes I think it's part of a spiritual awakening and no matter what I do in my life it will not seem enough because we must keep pressing forward onto completion doing His will, progressing and helping others. People say not to give negative thoughts words as it gives place to the devil to keep it happening in your life. I'm sick of starting over and being the new person at work. I have been alcohol free for over two and a half years and doing what I thought God wanted me to do but everything keeps changing. I got fired twice the second year that I was sober. I thought it was because my life was chaotic, yet no matter how hard I tried to make it stable. I tried to move in with the person I thought I was supposed to marry. I sold my house. I moved closer to work. I did overcome that; now four and a half years sober. It seemed like the better/nicer I was the meaner people were or the more obstacles that happened. I was beaten up and then fired. I was fired again for overstepping and doing what the doctor wanted without asking another department to do their job despite the fact that my preceptor told me to do the same thing the day before. I felt like I was doing what I was supposed to be doing. I told my manager that my preceptor didn't like me that day. She called a rapid response when she could have just deflated the blood pressure cuff and given oxygen or just removed the valve and given oxygen. I have thought that God didn't want me to work but if that was the case then why don't I have a surplus of money, so I don't have to worry about not working? Then I think, "Well, that is faith and what makes me a believer, knowing that He will provide no matter what." I hate the thought of not being able to pay for rent/bills or thinking that I must ask for help and maybe move into a government apartment and then what will others think. Sometimes it seems as if they go through life and have surplus, still with spouse, never any troubles with career such as like me almost losing my nursing license (or why do I have to prove myself)? Since I'm the one that denies my desires, lives life sober, attends church multiple times a week, listens to Christian music, don't watch bad stuff on TV. I have wondered, how do I promote God and the faith if my life doesn't look pleasing but like chaos and turmoil? I can now see that despite everything that I have lived through I always come out on top when I am obeying and trusting God. I know that there are times when I am in situations that I am overwhelmed because I did not know in whole, but I was protected, provided for and "safe" the entire time.

I have felt like others have been against me – like at work those that go out and drink. I believed that God would protect me and keep me from being oppressed, but right when things seemed to be going okay I was fired again. I felt like I should have changed jobs earlier that week as I received an offer, but I didn't accept because it was less money. I tried to explain that to TPAPN and others but still had my license get disciplinary action on it and posted in the Board of Nursing newsletter for the public and monitored an additional two years with drug tests despite constant sobriety. It was not that bad because I was able to maintain sobriety, but it was very stressful to have to remember to check in everyday and go somewhere and pee without over-drinking beverages and being diluted. Not to mention the cost and the ridicule at work, having to tell and leave shifts to go. Funny that they would think and talk badly about me, but they continued to drink with the false belief that somehow, I was an addict and they were "normal" so it was okay. Unless they know and just say/use that to make me feel worse or to stop drinking so that they can continue and justify their bad behavior, which is even worse. If you miss a day, it is the same as a dirty urine sample.

I don't understand why I can't just live a "normal" life with my kids, husband, go to work, shop eat, and live lovingly without adding more stressful things to an already stressful life.

I start my day with God, listening to the Bible or reading the one-year Bible. I speak a declaration CD and listen to worship music and praise. We must pray. Sometimes I hear God and doubt I am hearing Him. Sometimes I think that I have heard God but lost the things that I thought were Him or I think I deserve as His child or the bride of Christ. Why am I sitting in a stranger's house to make money (I was working nights as a pediatric home health nurse at the time). Why do "Christian" people come at me and say stuff to argue or make extra out of stuff that is small or insignificant? Why do extra work or try to make money if this is the case? Also, the more work that we do the more work that we make. I do believe in tithing, but I also hear so many preachers asking for money and supporting their families with it or even not supporting their families when they are living "right." With that being said, I get to where I am not sure where to tithe. Although, if that is us in another life then we should be nice to everybody because they are us. We are one body. Also, like when taking about not watching bad stuff maybe more than it goes in you but it transcends you to that a place or makes you go to a bad place in your life. Like Shutter Island or that Drinkwater movie. So, I was beat up by my boyfriend's other girlfriend and her mom. I didn't go to the hospital, but it was bad, like maybe traumatic brain injury. I thought that they were my mom and my aunt to this day. I worked in a psychiatric hospital for three years and coming to the end of that it was hard to function. I was drinking alcohol and had been beaten up, but even without that it was hard to function because I was seeing people as other people. It was like the system was broken and when people were calling people, I would know who they were as other people but couldn't say it. They were hurting me and making bad decisions, but I couldn't stop it. I am pending to go work at a prison. That is scary to me because it's like will I really be there or am I punished to have to go work there but really be free or am I privileged to go work with others in a serving manner like the police, to help God's others in prison to find God. Maybe they need my help because some of them shouldn't be there and people look at them as bad even though other people have done the same or worse. I used to think that I had relapsed and died and come back to life and had gone through all of that to meet Tony from Mercy Street, but we have been apart for three years so if that was the reason then why aren't we together now and why didn't we get married? Is it because he is bipolar, or because he didn't obey God and marry me, or is it because of this delusional life and I am stuck in these changing dimensions and I'm just in this martyr, scape-goat life with everyone looking bad at me but telling me to have faith that it is going to get better? How does it get better if this is my work? Hopefully I am wrong, and I am just going through something right now and people are right that it is hard because breakthrough is eminent. They say breakthrough is that something is about to end, and life is going to get better like not living bitter but get in the physical realm what you want. I think breakthrough is deliverance to another dimension but return to this one when time is right. Kind of like Groundhog Day but other realities going on at the same time. Keep doing the same thing over and over until get it right, like we are actors too.

I am going to pray about it (tithing). If I am right about all being one family, it is going to come back to me anyway (and it is coming back to me as proven in the past from God). Yet, again, why am I on the verge of being broke and not in surplus in my accounts? I declare in Jesus I am the head and not the tail, above and not beneath, the lender and not the borrower. If we are one, Alpha and Omega, then we are the head and the tail, above and beneath, the lender and the borrower. No one will ever steal from me again. I will know and be planted in my home church. I have been robbed since that statement. Church on the move, though? I'm not sure what I am supposed to be saying in this. It is hard to be open and honest and try to speak positively at the same time. I do not want my life to be chaotic or in turmoil, so I will never speak about this again. I'm glad that I was able to let you know, though. Although, upon editing and rereading this, fear is cropping up about being placed in a mental institution based on these thoughts. Instead, I hope that some of these thoughts resonate with someone and bring them out of oppression and give them hope and the strength to press on to a better life, so that they/you will know that they are above normal and don't ever let anyone make them/you think that you are crazy. That is a key sign of abuse and trying to control. Other bully moves that I have recognized lately are that they will say that you have no common sense or that they are laughing at you to get you to shut up exposing them.

Back to TPAPN PTSD, after my neuro-psych eval they sent me to after getting fired and making me pay $1,200.00 for it while not letting me work for the second time that year, they diagnosed me with several things, like PTSD and a history of a major depressive episode when I had tried to commit suicide in the 1990s. You are not forever your past. You are free from your past through Jesus' blood. We are supposed to move on from our pasts and make great lives. Don't let the enemy use things from your past to ruin your life today. Even something as huge as a major life-changing decision like that. Thank God, He allowed me to live. I know that He does not want to hold that against me forever to destroy my life but wanted me to learn and teach others that suicide does not work but only brings setbacks into your life. Anyways, my point to that is they want me to be productive and not have PTSD but fire me, not let me work, so how am I supposed to live not stressed, not want to give up? Believe that I am okay yet just diagnosed with mental health issues; also, even though they had already made me go through testing and be off work earlier in year for four months and diagnosed with anxiety which I admit to but have been praying against for years trying to trust in God and not worry. Pray over worry while enjoying life or resting while God takes care of our problems. Okay, back to the revelation. The neuropsychologist said that "no good deed goes unpunished" revelation was that I had to declare that my good deeds are never punished but rewarded in Jesus' Name. I will not return evil for good or start doing evil to prevent persecution. However, I expect love, understanding and help from my family and friends. I will continue to do good deeds for others.

We can't believe these lies/thoughts from the enemy. We must recognize and remember where they come from. We must know (have faith) that God is working it out for His and our good. It is a fine line that I must follow and continue to remember and pray throughout the day. So, God can guide me in everything that I do daily and help me to obey and make right decisions according to His will. I don't want to have to make what the world thinks are mistakes or bad decisions knowing it is what God wanted or must ask for financing for it or being rescued from it. I know that I might fail and might make mistakes in what I think is Him but what I am saying is when we get in trouble or things seem backwards but was what God needed done. I don't want to ever have to explain that to people that love me and know me. I want them to know that I am a good person and doing the will of God and be on board with what God is doing. I guess God has it for me to have to explain to them at times and to clarify stuff, but it is not enjoyable. I want to know how God wants things so I can cooperate with the Holy Spirit and know that what I am doing is His will and not question or doubt my hearing of His voice. See, I doubt myself but was just complaining about others doubting me. Maybe I mean that if I know that I know that God wanted something done. I want others to listen, understand, and believe me; not blame or punish me for doing what I was supposed to do. I can see where the BON is showing me accountable to others by doing all that they made me do (showing continued sobriety) but others see it on the surface as I am a bad person or not a competent nurse when in reality, I am just a law-abiding citizen that wants to fight crime and apparently be a martyr for Christ. I would much rather be an ambassador for Christ and speak positive, but others even condemn and look bad at others, talk bad about them. Example: Joel Osteen, even though he is highly favored by God, tries to refrain from sin and is a great speaker and a role model of being able to control your mouth, speak His word and live the blessed life people still persecute him. If he wasn't, God would not allow him to represent him.

There are times that I forgive others and then feel like why forgive them if they are going to continue in that behavior, or I forgive them and am willing to forgive them but then they bring up something that I have done and use that as a reason to keep a relationship away or an excuse for bad behavior. So, why should I forgive them if they don't even want me to?

My speech gets confused sometimes and then people misread me or accuse me of think things that I'm not or that might just cross my mind but aren't what I believe or what my final determination is. It's not okay for them to judge me saying I'm juding them. I must pause when asked a question to discern if they are speaking about something at face value or if they are trying to tell or ask me something on another level. Then there are those that complain, saying that they do all the work, although they like being the leader, and are being unappreciative of the actual humble, kinder worker. They are controlling and have the money and get recognition. I sometimes give them the benefit of the doubt, thinking that maybe they get confused and believe that the other is doing nothing or is actually stupid when in fact it the opposite. They might be knowledgeable of their actions and statements to achieve their outcome of having others do their work for them while they do what they want or nothing, while still looking like the competent one.

My father died a month ago. He had Alzheimer's. He was in a memory care unit in Livingston. My sister said that she would stay with him, and my mom and I left late at night. I had my first day at a new job the next morning. She didn't stay and he died alone. I got the call not even an hour later. I turned around and drove back, to no avail. At least I got to see him before she had him cremated. I had tried to talk him out of that in the past. I asked for some ashes to spread according to his wishes but she didn't allow me. I asked her about splitting his estate as was discussed that Christmas at her house prior to her trying to have my rights terminated and she said that he changed his mind at the end which was a lie. I am currently working with a three-year-old male as a pediatric home health nurse in Livingston (at the time that I wrote this). I went on an interview at a nursing home in the town that my father grew up in a couple of weeks ago. Some of these similarities make me think that there is more to all of this. Sometimes I think that he is still alive in others. He was in the Army in Vietnam. I had taken the kids a few times to visit him at the memory care facility. I wasn't allowed to take them to visit his last few years at home as I was told by my sister that the kids would stress him out. My sister didn't allow me to care for him even though I am a nurse. Now it is five years from the beginning of finding out that he had dementia, and it still torments me daily. I am hoping, praying, and believing for a release from this. The Word states that we will get back everything that has been stolen, in abundance. Who are we hiding from? Are we hiding from ourselves? How many systems are there? Why am I the only person in my family that had to be on welfare? Do I get a job and we all work together? Why did I get fired? Are we all together when we go to work, to church, any public place? Are we in different bodies? Are we one? Are we three? Why have I had to go through so many hard times? It appears others have had to go through nothing but basic life issues. I see basic life issues as the death of loved ones, moving, marriage etc. These now make me feel nothing. I hear that our life produces character in us. I believe that I had good character prior to all of my life turmoil. My life seems to be making me harder, less kind, less loving, as I have been abandoned and lost everything and everyone that I have loved, so I feel that I can't truly be happy and depend on anyone but God. I feel detached from everyone. I love my kids and my mom. There I times that I don't trust my mom or even believe that others are her sometimes but because she is my mom, I still call on her for help. I heard someone say to another that part of the phone is married to the mother board. I resonate with that. I feel my sister deeply betrayed me and for my mother to allow that makes it hard for me to trust her. I appreciate her being there for me now as opposed to her being against me in the past and aligning with my sister and the state to remove my kids from my custody when I was drinking alcohol and even after I quit, which

I sometimes see as a ploy to take my inheritance.
What is the purpose of making me less loving toward others? I thought that God is love. I don't want to be unkind or unloving. I want to be giving and trusting. I was told to trust no one, although I can't rely upon only myself. I think people are disillusioned in that they are self-sufficient even when they are gainfully employed or own businesses as they could lose it all instantly. People can be accused of things that they did not do. Anyone can go to prison at any time, even if living right, based on false accusations of others. These things scare me. That is not where I was going with that, though. I was more aimed at when people talk about people not working just because they do work as they could lose their jobs for reasons out of their control. I hate that I can't defend single moms or people on welfare just because it looks like I'm bitter. I can see the other side, that their husband or children's father didn't step up to the plate or was a danger to the kids but talk badly about them when they already got the short end of the stick. These people should feel blessed for what they have and not look down on others that might work harder than them and go through way more stuff than them if my theory is wrong. Because if these people that are married don't have to cycle through life, then it means then they have no idea about the hard life. We/I should not then be delusional and believe that they have had to go through anything like I have except then that I know that my life has been completely sabotaged and oppressed and made to look like it is my fault.
I can't even describe the tremendous loss I felt in love. Even when I had a husband it was like I didn't, as he talked about other women and made purposeful comments to hurt. I have had great hope in relationships and hoped beyond hope that they would last but didn't even make it to the altar. I thought the first one would kill me as I thought that his baby mom-

ma was just controlling him away from me and that we truly loved each other. The second man, I still think about multiple times a day, and it breaks my heart daily upon awakening. (Upon editing this is no longer the case, I go long periods of time without thinking about him). So, I guess that is three men that I truly thought were my husband. There was another that I lost listening to others advice and breaking up because we continued to argue, which I regret as I now know that is common in all marriages. (Upon editing I have found out that while I am hurt not having a husband or father for my children, it is best not to be with this man because he can't handle that I am busy and can't be at his beck and call. Although, I must work hard because I do want my children to enjoy their lives and to have the same lifestyle as a two-parent home). I have met another that said he was mature now and had learned from past relationships not to let it go bad only to do the exact same things that he said he didn't like in his past mate such as be controlling, insecure, and question the relationship (to the point of breaking it off then blaming the devil) instead of trusting God. I do want someone, and I do believe that God has someone for me, but I'm not sure why we aren't together except that he is still out there sinning, or he is being good, serving God and not searching for a woman. How do we trust after all we have been through, or are we destined to be apart in God's plan? God has given me the desire in my heart for my husband. So, I know that I will be married to him in the physical world, and we will be able to love each other like God, be each other's biggest fans, not be controlling, jealous, or abandon each other. We will trust each other, know that we are both working to serve God and others; we will not put each other down or make each other feel bad for working or doing what we believe we should be doing. We will encourage each other to rest and be understanding.

The moving on and on (encouraged by some in regards to dating) when there is conflict is from the devil and I will not believe in that to be made a sex slave to blatant sinning "Christian" men. We all sin and fall short, but sinning in thought and action are two different things. Sinning when you know is out and out a sin. Thoughts of sinning should be stopped there and will never grow into blatant sin. I will tithe and give money to the needy but not sow into those that I feel are oppressing me.

According to Psalm 100:3 (ESV), "Know that the Lord, He is God! It is He who made us, and we are His; we are His people and the sheep of His pasture." So, He can move us around and do whatever He likes with us and as long as we do His work, we will be okay. It might look bad, like standing strong on faith that we will retain our job when He might have to have us fired to move us. I would hope that I could hear His voice before and move accordingly but I question my decision making. Maybe I have been going after money too hard, but how am I supposed to support myself and children without working? Why would they want to take my license when I had so much care for others, going above and beyond, caring too much for patients? I didn't know the purpose of making me go through all of that or trying not to care about others anymore because I was in survival mode. That ended. I have to thrive as I am a child of God, and this is a promise. I will not live in fear but enjoy my life. All I know to do is not sin deliberately, pray, worship, try not to worry, read the Bible daily, and have personal time with God, seeking His will while listening to His voice. John 10:27 (ESV), "My sheep hear my voice, and I know them, and they follow me."
God has placed my children there for me to care for, but I need finances to do that and shouldn't have to be broke trying to buy for them to have a good life. We should all be able to

have a clean house and clothes, especially when we don't intentionally harm others, steal, kill or destroy but try to build up and lead in the way of life. A fruitful life of abundance and prosperity is the right way, which is so much better than the deceitful way. You don't have to lie to people or manipulate and try to control. A world where you can speak honestly to others and get them to do right according to God's will and not be mean or put others down in order to get them to do what you think is right. There are better ways. It should not make people feel good for others to feel bad. We should all be happy, confident, and live joyously together, not try to anger others or belittle them to make ourselves feel good. Competition is a mystery to me when we could ALL win!

Multiple Aha moments in every season "God speaking to me" confirming that wherever we go there we are or there are billions of people, and this is just God speaking to me but why would He speak to me in things that would trigger me? Why would He not want me at peace? The answer, I believe, is that sometimes we must get out of our comfort zones in order to keep going and do His will, maybe act out of character in order to accomplish what needs to be done.

We are to make disciples and help others to live according to God's ways so they can have the blessed life, Deuteronomy 28, 29, & 30, versus living a cursed life. God rains on the just and the unjust.

There are those that serve God and rely on tithes and gifts to continue but are there those that just use God's Word and this knowledge to make money instead of helping others. I believe that encouraging others is helping them, but we also need money to live and physical help.
Faith over fear: it can wax and wane, but we must push

through and obey anyway despite the fear arising, as fear brings about more fear and can keep or postpone the best from happening. All things are permissible but not all things are beneficial.

We must push on as we will always have enemies, but we must know that we always have the victory no matter what because of who we are and whose we are.

We must believe and not doubt. The truth is Jesus = (The Word). Our standard is to judge everything, to check what is right and wrong, then make decisions. We are called believers because we believe (and do not doubt). We believe not only in Jesus but in living by faith and not giving up daily (even moment by moment or circumstance by circumstance). We don't quit even when we hear bad news, when we want out of difficult circumstances, away from people that we don't get along with, or hard jobs. We are to fight through those thoughts, doubts, fear and/or anger so we can be the light and in return our life and theirs will be better.

Do something today that your future self will be proud of. Let go of what is not good so that you can get what is better. Even if you are not ready to completely let go you can let go and give it to God so that you don't have to worry about it but let God fight for you and if it is meant to be then it will be bit. You can relax in letting God have it and you don't have to stress about it, what to do about it, make a decision about it Just let go – pray, give it to Him, lay it down by giving Him the responsibility of taking care of it the best way. This allows you to relax and enjoy life even when you aren't sure about something or know exactly what needs to be done but don't know how to do it. He knows how to make it better either way.

We rest. When we rest, He works. The battle is His.
Also, this is why forgiveness is important, because we must be happy for others getting the best from God as we all prosper from His plan. Bless our enemies and pray for those who persecute us! Forgive at a distance because they may never change and allow the enemy to continue to use them. But believe and pray for them to be set free and their eyes opened wide to God and desire to do His plan/will from this day forward.

Don't doubt during trials and tribulations/testing. Remember that the future is better. Stay positive and don't return to bad habits or negative people because you might have to go through all of the hard thing again to learn. BThere is also grace, but if God wants you somewhere doing something you will make it just your choice on the hard way or easy way and how long do you want it to take to receive your BLESSED LIFE- desires of your heart- best destiny (the life God has planned for you). Stay loving to others, doing good even when you can't see these changes. God is working.
We praise- spiritual warfare. Other forms of spiritual warfare are mentioned later.

Commanding Angels with God's word. Our words spoken of God's Word are as powerful as when God speaks to them.
Speaking in tongues to edify self – we have to take care of ourselves to be able to help others.

Black letters are from God – God talking in red letters is Jesus- the rest of the Word was inspired by God.

When you see somebody get something, if that triggers jealousy- don't let it. Remember to turn that into being happy for them and pray that you receive it or what you want. Whatever we see others being blessed with we can be blessed with too.

Our Father owns everything; don't put limits on what you are believing for yourself- believe big, dream big- if you hear of someone being blessed be happy for them and thank God that you receive it too. Vision- if you believe you will receive. Although there are thorns in our side to keep us in line with His will and character, it can also be fluid depending on what is going on or needs to be done.

According to Ephesians chapter one, we are God's holy people, faithful followers of Christ. May God our Father and the Lord Jesus Christ give us grace and peace. We can yell out grace and peace and call them in. We should give praise to the Father of our Lord Jesus Christ who has blessed us with every spiritual blessing in the heavenly realms because we are united with Christ. God loved us and chose us in Christ before He even made the world. God is rich in kindness and grace, and we bring Him much pleasure by being in His family. God purchased our freedom and forgave our sins by His Son's blood. The mystery of Christ revealed to us by God is to fulfill His own good plan. At the right time He will bring everything from heaven and earth together with His Son as the authority. Since we are united with Christ, we have received an inheritance from God and He makes everything work out according to His plan. We are to trust God and bring Him praise and glory. When we believe in Christ he identifies us as His own by giving us the Holy Spirit. The Spirit is God's guarantee that He will give us our promised inheritance. Again, we are to praise and glorify Him. We are to have strong faith in the Lord and LOVE people. Love with action as in 1 Corinthians 13, being all the fruits of the spirit listed in Galatians 5. He gives us spiritual wisdom and insight and grows us in His knowledge. Our hearts are flooded with light, and we understand the confident hope that He gave us. We understand the greatness of God's mighty power even to raise the dead.

# Chapter Two
# Ephesians

Ephesians 2:4-10 (NLT) But God is so rich in mercy, and He loved us so much, that even though we were dead because of our sins, he gave us life when he raised Christ from the dead. (It is only by God's grace that you have been saved!) For He raised us from the dead along with Christ and seated us with Him in the heavenly realms because we are united with Christ Jesus. So, God can point us in all future ages as examples of the incredible wealth of His grace and kindness toward us, as shown in all He has done for us who are united with Christ Jesus. God saved you by His grace when you believed. And you can't take credit for this; it is a gift from God. Salvation is not a reward for the good things that we have done, so none of us can boast about it. For we are God's masterpiece. He has created us anew in Christ Jesus, so we can do the good things he planned for us long ago."

We were brought near to God through Jesus' blood. He broke down the wall of hostility. Eph 2:13-21 (NLT) But now you have been brought united with Christ Jesus. Once you were far away from God, but now you have been brought near to Him through the blood of Christ. For Christ himself has brought peace to us. He united Jews and Gentiles into one people when, in his own body on the cross, he broke down the wall of hostility that separated us. He did this by ending the system of law with its commandments and regulations. He brought the good news of peace to you Gentiles who were far away from Him, and peace to the Jews who were near. Now all of us can come to the Father through the same Holy Spirit because of what Christ has done for us. So now you

Gentiles are no longer strangers and foreigners. You are citizens with all of God's Holy people. You are members of God's family. Together we are His house, built on the foundation of the Apostles and Prophets. The Cornerstone is Christ Jesus himself. We are carefully joined together in Him, becoming a holy temple for the Lord. Through Him we are also being made part of this dwelling where God lives by His spirit.
Ephesians 3:6-7 (NLT) "And this is God's plan: Both Gentiles and Jews who believe the Good News share equally in the riches inherited by God's children. Both are part of the same body, and both enjoy the promise of blessings because they belong to Christ Jesus." By God's grace and mighty power, we are given the privilege to serve him by spreading this Good News.

Therefore, we have endless treasures available to us despite our undeservedness. The secret was that God's purpose was to use the church to display His wisdom. So, we can come boldly and confidently into God's presence. An example of prayer that we should use is that Paul prayed (on his hands and knees) for inner strength from His spirit, that Christ will make His home in our hearts as we trust in Him and obtain understanding of His deep love for us.

Ephesians 3:19-21 (NLT) "May you experience the love of Christ, though it is too great to understand fully. Then you will be made complete with all the fullness of life and power that comes from God. Now all glory to God, through His mighty power, at work in us, He will accomplish infinitely more than we might ask or think. Glory to Him in the church and in Christ Jesus through all generations forever and ever! Amen."

Ephesians 4:2-6 (NLT) "Always be humble and gentle. Be

patient with each other, making allowance for each other's faults because of your love. Make every effort to keep yourselves united in the Spirit, binding yourselves together with peace. For there is one body and one spirit, just as you have been called to one glorious hope for the future. There is one Lord, one faith, one baptism, one God and Father of all, who over all, in all, and living through all."

Ephesians 4: 11-16 (NLT) "Now these are the gifts Christ gave to the church: the apostles, the prophets, the evangelists, the pastors and teachers. Their responsibility is to equip God's people to do His work and build up the church, the body of Christ. This will continue until we all come to such unity in our faith and knowledge of God's Son that we will be mature in the Lord, measuring up to the full and complete standard of Christ. Then we will no longer be immature like children. We won't be tossed and blown about by every wind of new teaching. We will not be influenced when people try to trick us with lies so clever, they sound like the truth. Instead, we will speak the truth in Love, growing in every way more and more like Christ, who is the head of His body, the Church. He makes the whole body fit together perfectly. As each part does its own special work, it helps the other parts grow, so that the whole body is healthy and growing and full of love." Do not wander from the life God gives. Ephesians 4:17-32 (NLT) "With the Lord's authority I say this: Live no longer as the Gentiles do, for they are hopelessly confused. Their minds are full of darkness; they wander far from the life God gives because they have closed their minds and hardened their hearts against him. They have no sense of shame. They live for lustful pleasure and eagerly practice every kind of impurity. But that isn't what you learned about Christ. Since you have learned about the truth that comes from Him, throw off your old sinful nature and former way of life corrupted by lust and deception. Instead, let the Spirit renew your thoughts and attitudes. Put on your new nature, created to be God like- truly righteous and holy. So stop telling lies. Let us tell our neighbor the truth, for we are all parts of the same body. And don't sin by letting anger control you. Don't let the sun go down while you are still angry, for anger gives a foothold to the devil. If you are a thief, quit stealing, use your hands for good hard work and then give generously to those in need. Don't use foul or abusive language. Let everything that you say be good and helpful, so that your words will be an encouragement to those who hear them. And do not bring sorrow to God's Holy Spirit by the way you live. Remember, He has identified you as His own, guaranteeing that you will be saved on the day of redemption. Get rid of all bitterness, rage, anger, harsh words and slander, as well as all types of evil behavior. Instead, be kind to each other, tenderhearted, forgiving one another, just as God through Christ has forgiven you."

Ephesians 5:1-33 (NLT) "Imitate God, therefore in everything you do, because you are his dear children. Live a life filled with love, following the example of Christ. He loved us and offered himself as a sacrifice for us, a pleasing aroma to God. Let there be no sexual immorality, impurity or greed among you. Such sins have no place among God's people. Obscene stories, foolish talk, and coarse jokes- these are not for you. Instead let there be thankfulness to God. You can be sure that no immoral, impure, or greedy person will inherit the Kingdom of Christ and of God. For a greedy person is an idolater, worshipping the things of this world. Don't be fooled by those who try to excuse these sins, for the anger of God will fall on all who disobey him. Don't participate in the things these people do. For once you were full of darkness, but now you have light from the Lord. So live as people of light! For this light within you produces only what is good and right and true. Carefully determine what pleases the Lord. Take no part in the worthless deeds of evil and darkness; instead, expose them. It is shameful even to talk about the things that ungodly people do in secret. But their evil intentions will be exposed when the light shines on them, for the light makes everything visible. This is why it is said, 'Awake, O sleeper, rise up from the dead, and Christ will give you light.' So be careful how you live. Don't live like fools, but like those who are wise. Make the most of every opportunity in these evil days. Don't act thoughtlessly but understand what the Lord wants you to do. Don't be drunk with wine, because that will ruin your life. Instead, be filled with the Holy Spirit, singing psalms and hymns and spiritual songs among yourselves, and making music to the Lord in your hearts. And give thanks for everything to God the Father in the name of our Lord Jesus Christ. And further, submit to one another out of reverence for Christ. For wives, this means submit to your husbands as to the Lord. For a husband is the head of his wife as Christ is the head of the church. He is the Savior of his body, the church. As the church submits to Christ, so you wives should submit to your husbands in everything. For husbands, this means love your wives, just as Christ loved the church. He gave up his life for her to make her holy and clean, washed by the cleansing of God's word. He did this to present her to himself as a glorious church without a spot or wrinkle or any other blemish. Instead, she will be holy and without fault. In the same way, husbands ought to love their wives as they love their own bodies. For a man who loves his wife actually shows love for himself. No one hates his own body but feeds and cares for it, just as Christ cares for the church. And we are members of his body. As the Scriptures say, 'A man leaves his father and mother and is joined to his wife, and the two are united into one.' This is a great mystery, but it is an illustration of the way Christ, and the church are one. So again I say, each man must love his wife as he loves himself, and the wife must respect her husband."

# Chapter Three
# Transformation

Renew your mind.

Be yet transformed by the renewing of your mind. Renew your mind- each time you start to think badly about your past or circumstances or doubting God- reframe your mind by seeking God- pray- read the Word- meditate (seek His face).

Be ye transformed by the renewing of your mind. God's Word is now in our heart (New Testament) Jesus died for us and gave us the Holy Spirit.

## 1. First: Will It

God's will is always good/perfect.
"Work hard so you can present yourself to God and receive his approval. Be a good worker, one who does not need to be ashamed and who correctly explains the word of truth. a workman that need not to be ashamed, rightly dividing the word of truth." (2 Timothy
The truth is the origin of all increase.

## 2. Then: Say It.

For with the heart one believes and is justified, and with the mouth one confesses and is saved (Romans 10:8 ESV).

Just because you said it doesn't mean that you believe. If you are unsure:

Keep speaking it until it gets down in your Heart (spirit man) it will then become faith and you will believe.
The manifestation of what your heart desires will appear/ happen in your life.

Faith always comes by hearing.
Preach to yourself.
Speak faith confessions every day; you hear them when you speak them.
"Truly, I say unto you, whoever says to this mountain, Be taken up and thrown into the sea, and does not doubt in his heart, but believes that what he says will come to pass, it will be done for him (Mark
We have what we believe and say!!! Angels move at least at the speed of light and do what we say, harkening to the voice of His Word.
His Word spoken from our mouths will never return void.
We have ordained strength out of our mouth.

Great Faith
Faith-hope-love
"So now faith, hope, love abide, these three: but the greatest of these is love."

"For we which have believed do enter into rest, as he said, As I have sworn in my wrath if they shall enter into my rest: although the works were finished from the foundation of the world." Hebrews
Great faith always manifests!!!
Powerful people loving God- Jesus loves people.
Jesus came to do away with religion and bring us power.
Tongues edify me- speaking to God- He understands.
I want whatever God wants me to have.
Pure heart- not religious eyes

I want to be everything God wants me to be and do everything God wants me to do.
Say, "Yes, Lord."
Pray for those who don't believe the same as you.
Seek the Lord!
"The young lions do lack, and suffer hunger: but they that seek the Lord shall not want any good thing" (Psalms

"And when Jesus was entered into Capernaum, there came unto him a centurion, beseeching him, And saying, Lord, my servant lieth at home sick of the palsy, grievously tormented. And Jesus saith unto him, I will come and heal him. The centurion answered and said, Lord, I am not worthy that thou shouldest come under my roof: but speak the word only, and my servant shall be healed. For I am a man under authority, having soldiers under me: and I say to this man, Go, and he goeth; and to another, Come, and he cometh; and to my servant, Do this, and he doeth it. When Jesus heard it, he marvelled, and said to them that followed, Verily I say unto you, I have not found so great faith, no, not in Israel. And I say unto you, That many shall come from the east and west, and shall sit down with Abraham, and Isaac, and Jacob, in the kingdom of heaven. But the children of the kingdom shall be cast out into outer darkness: there shall be weeping and gnashing of teeth. And Jesus said unto the centurion, Go thy way; and as thou hast believed, so be it done unto thee. And his servant was healed in the selfsame hour."

1. Seek God first - with all your heart
This means to seek Him more than a house/car (whatever you desire most). He will then give you these things
I can do without anything, although I cannot do/be anything without God.
"Seek the Kingdom of God above all else, and live righteous-

ly, and He will give you everything you need. So don't worry about tomorrow, for tomorrow will bring its own worries. Today's trouble is enough for today." (Matthew
You will find Him.
"I love them that love me. Those who search will surely find me" (Proverbs
Riches and honor are with God.
"Riches and honor are with me, enduring wealth and righteousness" (Proverbs
"I sought the Lord, and he answered me, and delivered me from all my fears" (Psalm

~Don't make Him #2 in your day.
"But seek first the kingdom of God and all His righteousness and all these things shall be added unto you." (Matthew 6:33, NKJV).

2. Don't be afraid to talk to the right people about the problem- we need help.
First fruit (read bible/pray first thing in the morning) then the rest of your day is holy.
"For if the firstfruit be holy, the lump is also holy: and if the root be holy, so are the branches" (Romans
Holy One of Israel.
The Lord says: you shall seek me and find me!!!!
"And ye shall seek me, and find me, when ye shall search for me with all your heart" (Jeremiah
"Thus says the Lord, your Redeemer, the Holy One of Israel: I am the Lord your God who teaches you to profit, who leads you by the way that you should go" (Isaiah

Love from your heart and not the flesh.
Greet people with friendliness.
Respect and honor others.

We are blessed with glory and wealth.
We are God's! We are God's!
Respect and love people
Do not be afraid from your past trauma; only fear the Lord.
We will live and not die. We will declare the Lord in land of the living.
We have a covenant with God. We are lions.

Psalm 1:1 NLT states that we will have joy if we do not take advice from the wicked, stand around with sinners, or join with mockers.
We will also not be a stumbling block for anyone.
Call things that be, not as though they are, but how you want them to be.
God has delivered us from the powers of darkness (addiction, victimization, oppression). We have been translated into the kingdom.
"For he has rescued us from the kingdom of darkness and transferred us into the kingdom of his dear Son, who purchased our freedom and forgave our sins." (Colossians
Let nothing cause us fear or intimidation.
Let nothing and no one trigger us.
We will not allow others' words to upset us, because we know who we are in Christ.
We shall not let them upset us. We will stive for peace in ourselves and with others. Proverbs 26:4 NLT says, "Don't answer the foolish arguments of fools, or you become as foolish as they are." We will bow down to nothing.
We will win and never lose.

3. Always ask God's will
Ask and it will be given.
2 Corinthians 1:20 NLT, "For all of God's promises have been fulfilled in Christ with a resounding 'Yes!' And through

Christ, our 'Amen' (which means 'Yes') ascends to God for his glory."
He will not say no to His will.
His will is that I know the enemy's schemes and plans.
His will is that I have the desires of my heart.
His will is that I have joy and not sorrow.
His will is to HEAL!

4. Speak the word only
"Therefore, the Lord, the God of Israel says: I promised that your branch of the tribe of Levi would always be my priests. But I will honor those who honor me, and I will despise those who think lightly of me." (1 Samuel
Honor is the value that we place. We esteem Him higher and greater than anyone or anything else.
"Honor the Lord with thy substance, and with the first fruits of all thine increase." (Proverbs
So shall your barns be filled with plenty.
He placed Hhimself under authority.
The only way to have authority is to be under authority.
Honor others and pray for them.
We get to honor Him.
Clarity about work:
I am believing for life, although heaven is much better place.
Speak with the ones who have authority.
Peace.
Joy.
The body is one.

1 Corinthians 12:12 NLT "The human body has many parts, but the many parts make up one whole body. So it is with the body of Christ."
Messages from the body are sent to the head then the head processes and sends back down what is needed.

5. Great faith always obeys God
"After this he went down to Capernaum, he, and his mother, and his brethren, and his disciples: and they continued there not many days."

"If you will only obey me, you will have plenty to eat." (Isaiah Faith should never allow doubt; do not hesitate, speak the Word and do not question it. We do not have to know how God is going to do it but we will see the manifestations.

Believe God.
There are no limits/time/distance to great faith.
We can and will get what God has for us.
If we believe in our heart and confess out of our mouths, we will believe it in our hearts and get what we believe for!

We have the power of life and death in our tongue. Faith comes by hearing.
Confessions/declarations: speak them in the now!
This is a day that the Lord has made. I will rejoice and be glad in it...Everyday!
Increase me more and more, me and my children.
I am always in the right place at the right time.
I have the miracle and the living Word of God in me; I am victorious!
The Lord is my Shepherd, and I shall not lack or want.
I have great faith! Your head will listen to your mouth.
The speech center will change your whole body!

There is hope for:
Healing
Deliverance

## Blessings

When you have a bad thought, put your hand over your mouth (so that you don't say it). Some things that are done in darkness you should never even mention in light. Every word that you speak is a seed that you sow. If you want to shut the door on the past so that it will not affect you today or ever, then repent, wash under the Blood, and never mention it again.

There is a Kingdom way of living and a Babylonian way of living. We should do things according to God's will and not just for money, but realize that others are doing things for money. Satan uses people at work or the government to try to distract you from doing God's will.

We are Christ's ambassadors.

We are not of the world; we are going through this barren land. Be enemies with the world.

Live, walk, and talk like we belong to the kingdom of heaven.

Our spiritual family are those who do the will of our Father.

There is only one outcome to the good fight of faith. We WIN

"We love to change." We can change. We do not intentionally offend others and we are not offended easily. We are polite and communicate in a way that does not offend others.

We communicate with God face-to-face by going into prayer and into His presence. When we talk face-to-face with God in His presence, He will go through whatever is necessary to get to where we are. We can always count on Him.

There are "friends" who destroy each other, but a real friend sticks closer than a brother (Proverbs

Right People

When we pick the wrong friend then we end up in the wrong place. You can't pick a wrong friend and think that everything will be okay.

Don't be fooled by those who say such things, for 'bad company corrupts good character.' Think carefully about what is right and stop sinning. For to your shame, I say that some of you don't know God at all" (1 Corinthians
Stay clear of temptation. Don't get upset when heathens act like Satan; be mad when Christians don't act like Christ. Another biblical example is Peter: the wrong company (people) will make you deny Jesus. People with bad attitudes and/or that cuss will cause you to be negative and cuss too. Although do not be alone for too long either, be around people that will encourage you, lift you up and pray for/with you. You need to come together with other people, but come together with the right people. Spend time with those that spend time with Jesus. Those that love you. Those who give a right word.
Don't listen to people that tell you not to go to church. Hebrews 10:25 NLT says: "And let us not neglect our meeting together, as some people do, but encourage one another, especially now that the day of His return is drawing near."
Do not send children to be alone when in trouble because the devil will antagonize them.
"For God has not given us a Spirit of fear and timidity, but of power, love and self-discipline" (2 Timothy 1:7 NLT). We must learn to be comfortable even when in uncomfortable situations.

Be prepared to receive.
We give God all the glory, honor, and the praise; we get the victory.

God is the Creator.
Satan does not create; he prevents.
If you seek His face, He will find you and grab you out.

Deliverance

"And who was it who rebelled against God, even though they heard his voice? Wasn't it the people Moses led out of Egypt? And who made God angry for forty years? Wasn't it the people who sinned, whose corpses lay in the wilderness? And to whom was God speaking when he took an oath that they would never enter his rest? Wasn't it the people who disobeyed him? So, we see that because of their unbelief they were not able to enter his rest." (Hebrews
Unbelief brings no rest.
Cast down the enemy before he creeps into your house.

"The night is almost gone; the day of salvation will soon be here. So, remove your dark deeds like dirty clothes, and put on the shining armor of right living. Because we belong to the day, we must live decent lives for all to see. Don't participate in the darkness of wild parties and drunkenness, or in sexual promiscuity and immoral living, or in quarreling and jealousy. Instead, clothe yourself with the presence of the Lord Jesus Christ. And don't let yourself think about ways to indulge your evil desires" (Romans

You can't put armor on until you cast down works of darkness in your own heart and life. Examine yourself. Put on the armor right after ridding yourself of sin. Check yourself according to the Word. Confess sins but don't allow that to condemn you.

Put on the armor everyday:
"Put on all of God's armor so that you will be able to stand firm against all strategies of the devil. For we are not fighting against flesh-and-blood enemies, but against evil rulers and authorities of the unseen world, against mighty powers in this dark world, and against evil spirits in the heavenly places. Therefore, put on every piece of God's armor so you

will be able to resist the enemy in the time of evil. Then after the battle you will still be standing firm. Stand your ground, putting on the belt of truth and the body armor of God's righteousness. For shoes, put on the peace that comes from the Good News so that you will be fully prepared. In addition to all of these, hold up the shield of faith to stop the fiery arrows of the devil. Put on salvation as your helmet, and take the sword of the Spirit, which is the word of God. Pray in the Spirit at all times and on every occasion. Stay alert and be persistent in your prayers for all believers everywhere. And pray for me, too. Ask God to give me the right words so I can boldly explain God's mysterious plan that the Good News is for Jews and Gentiles alike" (Ephesians

"So now there is no condemnation for those who belong to Christ Jesus. And because you belong to him, the power of the life-giving Spirit has freed you from the power of sin that leads to death" (Romans

.

Walk not after the flesh but in the spirit.
The Word is authority!
I owe no man anything but to love him!!!
It's not me doing it; it's God. It's me speaking but God doing it.

Tell the angels to do the Word - declare the Word.
Man shall love good by the fruit of your mouth; by the increase of your lips, you shall be satisfied.
Reinforce your faith.
When the angels do the works, it's God doing the work, although He stays on the throne.
I am righteous.
Don't let condemnation take your righteousness.

Proverbs 23:7 NKJV
“For as a man thinks in his heart, so is he.”

It’s our responsibility to make sure that our heart is not troubled.
Don’t end something in the natural that you started in the spiritual.
It’s nothing to do with me; quit trying to fix it myself - let go and let God.
Stop worrying about it.
Like, don’t reach out to people - God does it without having to talk to others and trying to work for it.
Don’t try to figure it out.
Just rule and reign.
God is going to tell us to do something- let Him get credit for it- we have victory.
Relax.
Quit sweating it.
Start using your faith, not your back; don’t struggle!
Righteousness.
We are ruling in life.
Go from struggling to ruling and reigning!

Work by speaking.
It is work to speak the right thing and to use your faith.
Say what you want to happen and say it until you see it..
Righteousness.
We are born into true holiness and righteousness.
YOU ARE PURE.

Judge yourself correctly but do not condemn yourself.
“But if we confess our sins to him, he is faithful and just to forgive us from all wickedness” (1 John 1:9 NLT).
We are righteous again.

“Therefore, there is NOW no condemnation for those who are in Christ Jesus” (Romans 8:1 NLT).

“Don’t let your hearts be troubled. Trust in God, and trust also in me. There is more than enough room in my Father’s home. If this were not so, would I have told you that I am going to prepare a place for you?” (John

Every day is 1,000 years; 1,000 years is a day.
Everybody is young - no hair dye needed.
“We are confident, yes, well pleased rather to be absent from the body and to be present with the Lord.” (2 Corinthians 5:8 NKJV)
“For the trumpet will sound, and the dead will be raised incorruptible, and we shall be changed. For this corruptible must put on incorruption, and this mortal must put on immortality” (1 Corinthians 52b-53 NKJV).

We are the bride of Christ.
We are the body of Christ.
The ecclesia, the church, when we all come to the same place “The called out ones.”
The church is a group of people that are called out.
So, God can come and do what He wants to.
We should be having such a good life and living heaven on earth. So, we don’t even pay attention to the hell that we are going through.

Christ is our refuge.
“Those who live in the shelter of the Most High will find rest in the shadow of the Almighty. This I declare about the Lord: He alone is my refuge, my place of safety; he is my God, and I trust him. For he will rescue you from every trap and protect

you from deadly disease. He will cover you with his feathers. He will shelter you with his wings. His faithful promises are your armor and protection. Do not be afraid of the terrors of the night, nor the arrow that flies in the day. Do not dread the disease that stalks in darkness, nor the disaster that strikes at midday. Though a thousand fall at your side, though ten thousand are dying around you, these evils will not touch you. Just open your eyes and see how the wicked are punished. If you make the Lord your refuge, if you make the Most High your shelter, no evil will conquer you; no plague will come near your home. For he will order his angels to protect you wherever you go. They will hold you up with their hands, so you won't even hurt your foot on a stone. You will trample upon lions and cobras; you will crush fierce lions and serpents under your feet! The Lord says, 'I will rescue those who love me. I will protect those who trust in my name. When they call on me, I will answer; I will be with them in trouble. I will rescue and honor them. I will reward them with a long life and give them my salvation.'" (Psalm

"And since we have a great High Priest who rules over God's house, let us go right into the presence of God with sincere hearts fully trusting him. For our guilty consciences have been sprinkled with Christ's blood to make us clean, and our bodies have been washed with pure water. Let us hold tightly without wavering to the hope we affirm, for God can be trusted to keep his promise. Let us think of ways to motivate one another to acts of love and good works. And let us not neglect our meeting together, as some people do, but encourage one another, especially now that the day of his return is drawing near." (Hebrews
"He trusted in God; let him deliver him now, if he will have him: for he said, I am the Son of God. The thieves also, which were crucified with him, cast the same in his teeth. Now from

the sixth hour there was darkness over all the land unto the ninth hour. And about the ninth hour Jesus cried with a loud voice, saying, Eli, Eli, lama sabachthani? that is to say, My God, my God, why hast thou forsaken me? Some of them that stood there, when they heard that, said, This man calleth for Elias. And straightway one of them ran, and took a sponge, and filled it with vinegar, and put it on a reed, and gave him to drink. The rest said, Let be, let us see whether Elias will come to save him. Jesus, when he had cried again with a loud voice, yielded up the ghost. And behold, the veil of the temple was rent in twain from the top to the bottom; and the earth did quake, and the rocks rent; And the graves were opened; and many bodies of the saints which slept arose, And came out of the graves after his resurrection, and went into the holy city, and appeared unto many." (Matthew We live in Christ.

"For we know that since Christ was raised from the dead, he cannot die again: death no longer has mastery over him" (Romans 6: 9 ).

"But if the Spirit of Him that raised up Jesus from the dead dwell in you, He who raised Christ from the dead will also give life to your mortal bodies through His Spirit who dwells in you." (Romans

"My little children, these things write I unto you, that ye sin not. And if any man sin, we have an advocate with the Father, Jesus Christ the righteous: And he is the propitiation for our sins: and not for ours only, but also for the sins of the whole world. And hereby we do know that we know him, if we keep his commandments. He that saith, I know him, and keepeth not his commandments, is a liar, and the truth is not in him. But whoso keepeth his word, in him verily is the love of God perfected: hereby know we that we are in him. He that saith he abideth in him ought himself also so to walk, even as he walked. Brethren, I write no new commandment unto you, but an old commandment which ye had from the beginning. The old commandment is the word which ye have heard from the beginning. Again, a new commandment I write unto you, which thing is true in him and in you: because the darkness is past, and the true light now shineth. He that saith he is in the light, and hateth his brother, is in darkness even until now. He that loveth his brother abideth in the light, and there is none occasion of stumbling in him. But he that hateth his brother is in darkness, and walketh in darkness, and knoweth not whither he goeth, because that darkness hath blinded his eyes. I write unto you, little children, because your sins are forgiven you for his name's sake. I write unto you, fathers, because ye have known him that is from the beginning. I write unto you, young men, because ye have overcome the wicked one. I write unto you, little children, because ye have known the Father. I have written unto you, fathers, because ye have known him that is from the beginning. I have written unto you, young men, because ye are strong, and the word of God abideth in you, and ye have overcome the wicked one. Love not the world, neither the things that are in the world. If any man love the world, the love of the Father is not in him. For all that is in the world, the lust of the flesh, and the lust of the eyes, and the pride of life, is not of the Father, but is of the world. And the world passeth away, and the lust thereof: but he that doeth the will of God abideth for ever. Little children, it is the last time: and as ye have heard that antichrist shall come, even now are there many antichrists; whereby we know that it is the last time. They went out from us, but they were not of us; for if they had been of us, they would no doubt have continued with us: but they went out, that they might be made manifest that they were not all of us.

But ye have an unction from the Holy One, and ye know all things. I have not written unto you because ye know not the truth, but because ye know it, and that no lie is of the truth. Who is a liar but he that denieth that Jesus is the Christ? He is antichrist, that denieth the Father and the Son. Whosoever denieth the Son, the same hath not the Father: (but) he that acknowledgeth the Son hath the Father also. Let that therefore abide in you, which ye have heard from the beginning. If that which ye have heard from the beginning shall remain in you, ye also shall continue in the Son, and in the Father. And this is the promise that he hath promised us, even eternal life. These things have I written unto you concerning them that seduce you. But the anointing which ye have received of him abideth in you, and ye need not that any man teach you: but as the same anointing teacheth you of all things, and is truth, and is no lie, and even as it hath taught you, ye shall abide in him. And now, little children, abide in him; that, when he shall appear, we may have confidence, and not be ashamed before him at his coming. If ye know that he is righteous, ye know that every one that doeth righteousness is born of him." (1 John

"Rejoiceth not in iniquity, but rejoiceth in the truth; Beareth all things, believeth all things, hopeth all things, endureth all things. Charity never faileth: but whether there be prophecies, they shall fail; whether there be tongues, they shall cease; whether there be knowledge, it shall vanish away. For we know in part, and we prophesy in part. But when that which is perfect is come, then that which is in part shall be done away. When I was a child, I spake as a child, I understood as a child, I thought as a child: but when I became a man, I put away childish things. For now we see through a glass, darkly; but then face to face: now I know in part; but then shall I know even as also I am known. (1 Corinthians

We have more than enough all the time. We have the Prince of Peace!
We are seated with Him in heavenly places.
We have peace unspeakable.
We have victory EVERY DAY.
We are more than  conquerors.
We are symbols of Christ and a source of His blessings.
He defeated all grief and pain.

God's covenant:
"But this is the new covenant I will make with the people of Isreal after those days, "says the Lord. " I will put my instructions deep within them, and I will write them on their hearts. I will be theirn God, and they will be my people (Jeremiah 31:33, NLT).
"Remember the Lord your God. He is the one who gives you power to be successful, in order to fulfill the covenant, he confirmed to your ancestors with an oath." (Deuteronomy

"For the word of God is alive and powerful. It is sharper than the sharpest two-edged sword, cutting between soul and spirit, between joint and marrow. It exposes our innermost thoughts and desires." (Hebrews

"For he has rescued us from the kingdom of darkness and transferred us into the Kingdom of his dear Son, who purchased our freedom and forgave our sins" (Colossians

(1 John 4:18, NLT) "Such love has no fear, because perfect love expels all fear."
When we experience His perfect love, we will have no fear.
We are not free to say anything that we want to say. Cussing is giving the devil power to put you in bondage. The Word of God will help you above everything else.

Speak the TRUTH in love (even if it hurts others' hearts or feelings)
Be honest with yourself.
Don't put yourself in lack by going with the world's way of thinking if it's not the way of the Lord.

Let our will be His will, His way our way.
He won't go against our will. We need to not be religious in our thinking.
He wants all to be saved.
We need to stand up and be right; don't settle for what is wrong.

Jesus created a culture like heaven.
Strength from His Spirit helps us to overcome obstacles and to accomplish everything that we need to.
We are designed to prophesy.
We are to bring ourselves to the Lord often.
Don't hate on others; this is like asking God to hate on you.
The merciful shall receive mercy.
"God blesses those who are merciful, for they shall be shown mercy (Matthew 5:7 NLT)
Pray: Lord, help them. Lord, deliver them from that. Lord, have mercy on them.
"Getting wisdom is the wisest thing you can do! And whatever else you do, develop good judgment. (Proverbs 4:7, NLT).
Love God and love other people.

Our King is Jesus.
"The earth is the Lord's, and everything in it. The world and all its people belong to him." (Psalm 24:1 NLT)
"But I say, do not make any vows! Do not say, 'By heaven!' because heaven is God's throne. And do not say, 'By the earth!' because the earth is his footstool. And do not say, 'By Jeru-

salem!' for Jerusalem is the city of the great King." (Matthew
"What are mere mortals that you should think about them, human beings that you should care for them? Yet you made them only a little lower than God and crowned them with glory and honor."

"Give them this message for their masters: 'This is what the Lord of Heaven's Armies, the God of Israel, says: With my great strength and powerful arm I made the earth and all its people and every animal. I can give these things of mine to anyone I choose.'" (Jeremiah

The only thing that will make you genuinely happy (joyful) is doing exactly what God has called you to do (your purpose). Doing God's will brings you happiness.
He wants us to have it so that we can give.
Stay in His presence; do not faint in the face of adversity. He will strengthen us. Let the weak say "I'm strong." Stand and stand strong. Do not give up because of the way it looks or because someone gives you bad news, even if it's a doctor forecasting a terminal illness. There are miracle healings. Our God is Jehovah Ropha (our healer). Declare and believe for positive outcomes.
Bind the spirit (stroke, broken head, confusion, harassment, hard headedness).
You live and you declare the goodness of the Lord in the land of the living.
Whenever your peace is disturbed, it means that something needs to be done.
"I am leaving you with a gift, peace of mind and heart. And the peace I give is a gift the world cannot give. So don't be troubled or afraid." (John 14:27 NLT)
His peace He gave to me.
Let my heart not be troubled.

Don't let it stay one more day, not one more minute without fixing it.
Give and it shall be given unto me.

"You will live in joy and peace. The mountains and hills will burst into song, and the trees of the field will clap their hands! Where once there were thorns, cypress trees will grow. Where nettles grew, myrtles will sprout up. These events will bring great honor to the Lord's name; they will be an everlasting sign of his power and love." (Isaiah

"Blessed are the peacemakers for they shall be called the children of God (Matthew 5:9, NIV).

Walk in truth and love. We can speak a harsh truth gently with good intentions and a pure heart.
When your peace is broken spend some time with God.
Don't complain; don't be sad.

Truth is what God says it is and it lines up with the Word.

"You will keep in perfect peace all who trust in you, all whose thoughts are fixed on you! Trust in the Lord always, for the Lord GOD is the eternal Rock. He humbles the proud and brings down the arrogant city. He brings it down to the dust. The poor and oppressed trample it underfoot, and the needy walk all over it. But for those who are righteous, the way is not steep and rough. You are a God who does what is right, and you smooth out the path ahead of them."

Give it all to God and trust Him; it is easy.
If you don't have peace, no one around you will have peace.
Although, we still must go through tough stuff, we don't have to feel the weight of it because we gave it to God. Don't take

it back.
Whoever's hands it's in, they feel the weight of it, and the outcome is their responsibility.
Let problems go and turn them over to God. Trust Him. He is responsible. He is all knowing.
We are free. We don't have to be concerned with it. When the weight tries to come back, cast it off.
Learn to have peace; maintain peace in your life (in yourself).
We are not designed to carry sin's weight or things that break our hearts. That could break us. That's why Jesus died on the cross, so we do not have to bear it.

Strife is every evil thing.
The devil is the prince of confusion.
Jesus is the Prince of Peace!
We are the lender, not the borrower.
We are healthy, fit and appealing.
We can eat what we want to eat and maintain our ideal weight.
We are beautiful inside and out.
My needs are met according to His riches in glory.
-speak it and believe it-

In 1 Samuel 17:28, David's brother said that he was prideful (conceited). When we are aware of who we are, know the truth and act, sometimes it likes looks like pride to those who don't have Jesus or expect us to bow down to them.
Don't lie but speak faith. KNOW IT AND HAVE IT.

We know what God says so we can have it.
"And it is impossible to please God without faith. Anyone who wants to come to him must believe that God exists and that he rewards those who sincerely seek him" (Hebrews 11:6 NLT).

If you don't eat it in faith (if you still believe that it is dirty) then don't eat it.

Don't shack up. If you want to live with your significant other then get married.
???What is sex anyway??? You become one with the other!
What is kissing? You can become one by kissing.
Live the life; walk the walk.
Know the Word, be who God said you can be, and have what God said that you could have.
Don't let flesh take away your blessings.

"And so, dear brothers and sisters, I plead with you to give your bodies to God because of all he has done for you. Let them be a living and holy sacrifice—the kind he will find acceptable. This is truly the way to worship him. Don't copy the behavior and customs of this world, but let God transform you into a new person by changing the way you think. Then you will learn to know God's will for you, which is good and pleasing and perfect." (Romans

"But our High Priest offered himself to God as a single sacrifice for sins, good for all time. Then he sat down in the place of honor at God's right hand.

"For by that one offering he forever made perfect those who are being made holy. And the Holy Spirit also testifies that this is so. For he says, "This is the new covenant I will make with my people on that day, says the Lord: I will put my laws in their hearts, and I will write them on their minds." (Hebrews

"Then he says, 'I will never again remember their sins and

lawless deeds.' And when sins have been forgiven, there is no need to offer any more sacrifices. And so, dear brothers and sisters, we can boldly enter heaven's Most Holy Place because of the blood of Jesus. By his death, Jesus opened a new and life-giving way through the curtain into the Most Holy Place. And since we have a great High Priest who rules over God's house, let us go right into the presence of God with sincere hearts fully trusting him. For our guilty consciences have been sprinkled with Christ's blood to make us clean, and our bodies have been washed with pure water. Let us hold tightly without wavering to the hope we affirm, for God can be trusted to keep his promise."

Keep saying.
Keep believing!
Because HE is faithful.

"This is the message we heard from Jesus and now declare to you: God is light, and there is no darkness in him at all. So we are lying if we say we have fellowship with God but go on living in spiritual darkness; we are not practicing the truth. But if we are living in the light, as God is in the light, then we have fellowship with each other, and the blood of Jesus, his Son, cleanses us from all sin. If we claim we have no sin, we are only fooling ourselves and not living in the truth. But if we confess our sins to him, he is faithful and just to forgive us our sins and to cleanse us from all wickedness." (1 John

We are cleansed by the blood of the Lamb; ask for forgiveness when your conscience bothers you.

Enter God's rest. Hold fast to the promises for He is faithful. He will do it. He will show up and show off!

Don't hang around those that don't believe that the whole Bible is true.
The JUST will live by FAITH.
Walk away when people say stuff or rumors or anything. We are not trash compactors; don't let them plant seeds in you.
No hurting people jokingly. The devil doesn't care if you are playing. It's great to have fun and joke but not by hurting others.
Watch what you say. Your words are powerful.

If someone says that you are being prideful, examine yourself. Don't be bothered by it (don't get defensive) but be polite, apologize, and go on. Try not to let them upset you.
"Indeed, we all make many mistakes. For if we could control our tongues, we would be perfect and could also control ourselves in every other way. And among all the parts of the body, the tongue is a flame of fire. It is a whole world of wickedness, corrupting your entire body. It can set your whole life on fire, for it is set on fire by hell itself." (James

With your tongue you can control your whole body!!!!

"You want what you don't have, so you scheme and kill to get it. You are jealous of what others have, but you can't get it, so you fight and wage war to take it away from them. Yet you don't have what you want because you don't ask God for it. And even when you ask, you don't get it because your motives are all wrong—you want only what will give you pleasure."

"For verily I say unto you, That whosoever shall say unto this mountain, Be thou removed, and be thou cast into the sea; and shall not doubt in his heart, but shall believe that those things which he saith shall come to pass; he shall have whatsoever he saith. Therefore, I say unto you, What things soever ye desire, when ye pray, believe that ye receive them, and ye shall have them."

Believe that you receive what you ask for and you will have it.

***If it is italicized in the Bible then you can remove it and reread without that word.***
Ask for God's glory but not with the wrong motive.
All His promises are yes and amen.

We are polite.
We are kind.
We are not defensive; we do not allow others to trigger us.
We show the love of God to everybody and believe miracles for them. Just because we can see who they are and their motives does not mean that we have to show them who we are. We are greater than our opposition. If you don't know it, you will bend to them and react.

"Now the Lord is that Spirit: and where the Spirit of the Lord is, there is liberty. But we all, with open face beholding as in a glass the glory of the Lord, are changed into the same image from glory to glory, even as by the Spirit of the Lord." (2 Corinthians

Kanye West during a "talk" with Joel Osteen at Lakewood, discussed addiction, sex trafficking and drug dealing. We must light up the dark, reveal the bad, make believers, and bring people to Christ so that they can be saved, save others and be aware of the harm that they caused to themselves and others. So that they are not blinded by mere financial gain or the will to control others for evil. John Gray spoke of the realness of conversion the following Wednesday at Lakewood.

Fire is burning in our own community, neighborhood, schools, and jails. Start a ministry right in the middle of what the devil is doing. If you don't learn and live the Kingdom of God then you will die. Simple.
If others are not in the Kingdom, then those that appear to be friends are just leeches. In God's Kingdom, we are family, and EVERYBODY lives/THRIVES.
"And he said unto them, Unto you it is given to know the mystery of the kingdom of God: but unto them that are without, all these things are done in parables: That seeing they may see, and not perceive; and hearing they may hear, and not understand; lest at any time they should be converted, and their sins should be forgiven them. And he said unto them, Know ye not this parable? and how then will ye know all parables? The sower soweth the word" (Mark

The Kingdom operates by words.
You are going to be held accountable for every word, not just at the end of life going into Heaven, but day to day flows bring consequences. We have to control our thoughts, words and actions in order to bring about what we desire. In order to live our desired destiny, we must say what we want without complaining, teach others how to prosper, and live according to the blessings of God.

The devil will try and get you to use your words for his advantage- He will entice others to try and get you to think and speak negatively. Stay vigilant.

"And he said, So is the kingdom of God, as if a man should cast seed into the ground; And should sleep, and rise night and day, and the seed should spring and grow up, he knoweth not how. For the earth bringeth forth fruit of herself; first the blade, then the ear, after that the full corn in the ear. But when the fruit is brought forth, immediately he putteth in the sickle, because the harvest is come" (Mark

The closer we get to God, as our Kingdom increases, the less time it takes for our words to flourish and our prayers to be answered. We must live by praying, seeking clarity and direction from the Holy Spirit, so, that we may move forward with God's will and live life abundantly for ourselves and everyone around us.

He will reveal things to us by His Spirit. He has given us the earth. Don't let thoughts fail you, don't let your mouth fail you, don't let the devil deceive you by telling you that it's not going to happen.

Nobody hurts the children!
We don't offend!
We don't hurt anybody!
Don't talk badly about one another.

The church was designed to change you (for exactly what you are supposed to do/be) for your purpose.
Do not live under the curse.
"But Christ has rescued us from the curse pronounced by the law. When he was hung on the cross, he took upon himself the curse for our wrongdoing. For it is written in the scriptures, 'cursed is everyone who is hung on a tree.'" (Galatians 3:13 NIV)
Christ redeemed us from the curse that the blessing might fall.
Don't live in sin or by being the devil's puppet.

My people die because of the lack of knowledge. We have

knowledge, wisdom and understanding.
No weapon formed against us shall prosper. No weapon formed against our kids shall prosper. No weapon formed against our grandchildren shall prosper.
"The Lord will conquer your enemies when they attack you from one direction, but they will scatter from you in seven. The Lord will guarantee a blessing on everything that you do and will fill your storehouses with grain. The Lord your God will bless you in the land he is giving you" (Deuteronomy 28:7-8 NLT).

We entice them to serve the Lord because they want to be like us.
Love is the key.
Claim your authority.

"And it came to pass, that, as he was praying in a certain place, when he ceased, one of his disciples said unto him, Lord, teach us to pray, as John also taught his disciples. And he said unto them, When ye pray, say, Our Father which art in heaven, Hallowed be thy name. Thy kingdom come. Thy will be done, as in heaven, so in earth." (Luke

Let your conversation be without covetousness; be content. The lord will never leave you or forsake you. God is your helper. We are not alone.

They will see me not as a burden but as a blessing.
I will never lack. God hates lack. I am the lender, not the borrower. Always the head and never the tail. We are blessed coming into the city and going out of the city.
For your trouble, God will give you double of what you should have had!!!

Your character is what defines you! What people see in you. What honest people say about you.
Character is one of the distinguishing things that sets us apart. Be like God.
Walk like talk; be just like God- this is a God order.

# Chapter Four
# 10 Atributes of God

1. Understanding what a true father is like (a truly godly father)

2. Omniscient- all knowledge and understanding infinite- when our heart is condemning -God is greater than our heart and knows all things.

3. Omnipotent- able to do all things; He has no external limitations; nothing can restrain Him.

4. Omnipresence- all places at all times; His eyes are in every place. Selah- pause and think calmly about this.
"The Lord is watching everywhere, keeping his eye on both the evil and the good" (Proverbs 15:3 NLT).
God is unchanging; before anything was created God was. As sons we are not concerned [immutable].
"Before the mountains were born, before you gave birth to the earth and the world, from beginning to end, you are God" (Psalm 90:2 NLT).
"I am the Lord and I do not change. That is why you descendants of Jacob are not destroyed (Malachi 3:6 NLT).

5. Holy- Every encounter with God is holy; He can't accept or even look upon sin. 1 Samuel 2:2, NLT says, "No one is holy like the LORD! There is no one beside you: there is no ROCK like our God." Psalm 103:1, KJV: "Bless the Lord, O my soul; And all that is within me, bless His holy name!" Habakkuk 1:13a NLT says, "But you are pure and cannot stand the sight of evil." Psalm 96:9, NIV says "Worship the Lord in the splen-

dor of His holiness; tremble before him, all the earth."

6. Righteous- holiness manifested through righteousness (how expressed when dealing with others). Whoever pursues righteousness and kindness will find life, righteousness and honor. (Proverbs 21:21 ESV)

7. Gracious- ...The Lord is gracious, and full of compassion; Slow to anger, and of great mercy. The Lord is good to all: And his tender mercies are over all his works (Psalms 145:8-9, KJV).

8. Merciful- God not giving us what we deserve from sin. He has chosen salvation and deliverance to not keep us out of His presence. We are to endure forever.

9. Sovereign- free to do what's best for us; accept His leading. The devil is the accuser of the brethren. Men should treat their wives the way that God treats them, forgiving over and over, not staying angry. Forgive 70 times 70 every day.

10. Faithful - God is always going to show up- loving, watching, keeping, to turn my heart, to lead me in the path of righteousness.

"Jesus looked at them intently and said, 'Humanly speaking, it is impossible. But with God everything is possible'" (Matthew 19:26 NLT).

"For the word of God will never fail" (Luke 1:37 NLT)

Stop thinking in mind or flesh and start with God. With God, get in the face of Jesus, the presence of the Lord, let

His light shine. I want a man that's going to seek the face of Jesus. He will get it right because he's seeking the help that he needs. No pride; don't fall. With an open mind, behold and be changed when in the Lord's presence. From glory to glory we will have sweatless victories.
We must be like God. People are watching and depending on us. Be the answer to the trouble. Miracles and wonders are accomplished, and all needs are met according to His riches, so that we might minister to others, and it will be given back.

Be present, placed beside, close to Him. "I beseech you therefore, brethren, by the mercies of God, that you present your bodies as a living sacrifice, holy, acceptable to God, which is your reasonable service. And do not be conformed to this world, but be transformed by the renewing of your mind, that you may prove what is good and acceptable and perfect will of God." (Romans 12:1, NKJV)
Be willing and obedient.
In exchange we get money and power, although that is not what we are seeking. We are seeking to serve and do His will.
Arise.
"And so, dear brothers and sisters, I plead with you to give your bodies to God because of all he has done for you. Let them be a living and holy sacrifice- the kind he will find acceptable. This is truly the way to worship him" (Rom 12:1 NLT).

Submit- arrange under.
Obey.
Submitted to His will/way.
"But you belong to God, my dear children. You have already won a victory over those people, because the spirit who lives in you is greater than the spirit who lives in the world" (1 John 4:4 NLT).

Love has no fear, but perfect love expels all fear.
Experience His perfect love.
Experience- direct observation or participation in an event.
He is the potter, and we are the clay. We were designed to be.
Allow Him to mold us.
He is ready to put His glory on you. He will be so we can be.
He is all that we need.

#supposed to be kind, not tough.

"Let the people praise thee, O God; let all the people praise thee. Then shall the earth yield her increase; and God, even our own God, shall bless us. God shall bless us; and all the ends of the earth shall fear him" (Psalm
We only can sustain (kingdom prosperity) through GOD.
In the presence of God there is fullness of joy and in His right hand there is pleasure Fforever more.
"Thou wilt shew me the path of life: in thy presence is fulness of joy; at thy right hand there are pleasures for evermore" (Psalms
Don't try to figure it out; don't try to fix it myself.
The devil tries to ensnare us with words and thoughts.
We are the blessed and not the cursed.
The Word teaches us how to stay out of trouble and be blessed.

# Chapter Five
# Deuteronomy
## Chapters 28 and 29 NLT

Blessings Vs Cursings
Blessings for Obedience
28 If you fully obey the Lord your God and carefully follow all his commands I give you today, the Lord your God will set you high above all the nations on earth. 2 All these blessings will come on you and accompany you if you obey the Lord your God:
3 You will be blessed in the city and blessed in the country.
4 The fruit of your womb will be blessed, and the crops of your land and the young of your livestock—the calves of your herds and the lambs of your flocks.
5 Your basket and your kneading trough will be blessed.
6 You will be blessed when you come in and blessed when you go out.
7 The Lord will grant that the enemies who rise up against you will be defeated before you. They will come at you from one direction but flee from you in seven.
8 The Lord will send a blessing on your barns and on everything you put your hand to. The Lord your God will bless you in the land he is giving you.
9 The Lord will establish you as his holy people, as he promised you on oath, if you keep the commands of the Lord your God and walk in obedience to him. 10 Then all the peoples on earth will see that you are called by the name of the Lord, and they will fear you. 11 The Lord will grant you abundant prosperity—in the fruit of your womb, the young of your livestock and the crops of your ground—in the land he swore to your ancestors to give you.
12 The Lord will open the heavens, the storehouse of his

bounty, to send rain on your land in season and to bless all the work of your hands. You will lend to many nations but will borrow from none. 13 The Lord will make you the head, not the tail. If you pay attention to the commands of the Lord your God that I give you this day and carefully follow them, you will always be at the top, never at the bottom. 14 Do not turn aside from any of the commands I give you today, to the right or to the left, following other gods and serving them.

Curses for Disobedience

15 However, if you do not obey the Lord your God and do not carefully follow all his commands and decrees I am giving you today, all these curses will come on you and overtake you:

16 You will be cursed in the city and cursed in the country.

17 Your basket and your kneading trough will be cursed.

18 The fruit of your womb will be cursed, and the crops of your land, and the calves of your herds and the lambs of your flocks.

19 You will be cursed when you come in and cursed when you go out.

20 The Lord will send on you curses, confusion and rebuke in everything you put your hand to, until you are destroyed and come to sudden ruin because of the evil you have done in forsaking him.[a] 21 The Lord will plague you with diseases until he has destroyed you from the land you are entering to possess. 22 The Lord will strike you with wasting disease, with fever and inflammation, with scorching heat and drought, with blight and mildew, which will plague you until you perish. 23 The sky over your head will be bronze, the ground beneath you iron. 24 The Lord will turn the rain of your country into dust and powder; it will come down from the skies until you are destroyed.

25 The Lord will cause you to be defeated before your ene-

mies. You will come at them from one direction but flee from them in seven, and you will become a thing of horror to all the kingdoms on earth. 26 Your carcasses will be food for all the birds and the wild animals, and there will be no one to frighten them away. 27 The Lord will afflict you with the boils of Egypt and with tumors, festering sores and the itch, from which you cannot be cured. 28 The Lord will afflict you with madness, blindness and confusion of mind. 29 At midday you will grope about like a blind person in the dark. You will be unsuccessful in everything you do; day after day you will be oppressed and robbed, with no one to rescue you.

30 You will be pledged to be married to a woman, but another will take her and rape her. You will build a house, but you will not live in it. You will plant a vineyard, but you will not even begin to enjoy its fruit. 31 Your ox will be slaughtered before your eyes, but you will eat none of it. Your donkey will be forcibly taken from you and will not be returned. Your sheep will be given to your enemies, and no one will rescue them. 32 Your sons and daughters will be given to another nation, and you will wear out your eyes watching for them day after day, powerless to lift a hand. 33 A people that you do not know will eat what your land and labor produce, and you will have nothing but cruel oppression all your days. 34 The sights you see will drive you mad. 35 The Lord will afflict your knees and legs with painful boils that cannot be cured, spreading from the soles of your feet to the top of your head. 36 The Lord will drive you and the king you set over you to a nation unknown to you or your ancestors. There you will worship other gods, gods of wood and stone. 37 You will become a thing of horror, a byword and an object of ridicule among all the peoples where the Lord will drive you.

38 You will sow much seed in the field but you will harvest little, because locusts will devour it. 39 You will plant vineyards and cultivate them but you will not drink the wine or

gather the grapes, because worms will eat them. 40 You will have olive trees throughout your country but you will not use the oil, because the olives will drop off. 41 You will have sons and daughters but you will not keep them, because they will go into captivity. 42 Swarms of locusts will take over all your trees and the crops of your land.

43 The foreigners who reside among you will rise above you higher and higher, but you will sink lower and lower. 44 They will lend to you, but you will not lend to them. They will be the head, but you will be the tail.

45 All these curses will come on you. They will pursue you and overtake you until you are destroyed, because you did not obey the Lord your God and observe the commands and decrees he gave you. 46 They will be a sign and a wonder to you and your descendants forever. 47 Because you did not serve the Lord your God joyfully and gladly in the time of prosperity, 48 therefore in hunger and thirst, in nakedness and dire poverty, you will serve the enemies the Lord sends against you. He will put an iron yoke on your neck until he has destroyed you.

49 The Lord will bring a nation against you from far away, from the ends of the earth, like an eagle swooping down, a nation whose language you will not understand, 50 a fierce-looking nation without respect for the old or pity for the young. 51 They will devour the young of your livestock and the crops of your land until you are destroyed. They will leave you no grain, new wine or olive oil, nor any calves of your herds or lambs of your flocks until you are ruined. 52 They will lay siege to all the cities throughout your land until the high fortified walls in which you trust fall down. They will besiege all the cities throughout the land the Lord your God is giving you.

53 Because of the suffering your enemy will inflict on you during the siege, you will eat the fruit of the womb, the flesh

of the sons and daughters the Lord your God has given you. 54 Even the most gentle and sensitive man among you will have no compassion on his own brother or the wife he loves or his surviving children, 55 and he will not give to one of them any of the flesh of his children that he is eating. It will be all he has left because of the suffering your enemy will inflict on you during the siege of all your cities. 56 The most gentle and sensitive woman among you—so sensitive and gentle that she would not venture to touch the ground with the sole of her foot—will begrudge the husband she loves and her own son or daughter 57 the afterbirth from her womb and the children she bears. For in her dire need she intends to eat them secretly because of the suffering your enemy will inflict on you during the siege of your cities.

58 If you do not carefully follow all the words of this law, which are written in this book, and do not revere this glorious and awesome name—the Lord your God— 59 the Lord will send fearful plagues on you and your descendants, harsh and prolonged disasters, and severe and lingering illnesses. 60 He will bring on you all the diseases of Egypt that you dreaded, and they will cling to you. 61 The Lord will also bring on you every kind of sickness and disaster not recorded in this Book of the Law, until you are destroyed. 62 You who were as numerous as the stars in the sky will be left but few in number, because you did not obey the Lord your God. 63 Just as it pleased the Lord to make you prosper and increase in number, so it will please him to ruin and destroy you. You will be uprooted from the land you are entering to possess.

64 Then the Lord will scatter you among all nations, from one end of the earth to the other. There you will worship other gods—gods of wood and stone, which neither you nor your ancestors have known. 65 Among those nations you will find no repose, no resting place for the sole of your foot. There the Lord will give you an anxious mind, eyes weary

with longing, and a despairing heart. 66 You will live in constant suspense, filled with dread both night and day, never sure of your life. 67 In the morning you will say, "If only it were evening!" and in the evening, "If only it were morning!"—because of the terror that will fill your hearts and the sights that your eyes will see. 68 The Lord will send you back in ships to Egypt on a journey I said you should never make again. There you will offer yourselves for sale to your enemies as male and female slaves, but no one will buy you.

# Part Two
# Renewal of the Covenant (Blessings)

29 [b]These are the terms of the covenant the Lord commanded Moses to make with the Israelites in Moab, in addition to the covenant he had made with them at Horeb.
2 Moses summoned all the Israelites and said to them:
Your eyes have seen all that the Lord did in Egypt to Pharaoh, to all his officials and to all his land. 3 With your own eyes you saw those great trials, those signs and great wonders. 4 But to this day the Lord has not given you a mind that understands or eyes that see or ears that hear. 5 Yet the Lord says, "During the forty years that I led you through the wilderness, your clothes did not wear out, nor did the sandals on your feet. 6 You ate no bread and drank no wine or other fermented drink. I did this so that you might know that I am the Lord your God."
7 When you reached this place, Sihon king of Heshbon and Og king of Bashan came out to fight against us, but we defeated them. 8 We took their land and gave it as an inheritance to the Reubenites, the Gadites and the half-tribe of Manasseh.
9 Carefully follow the terms of this covenant, so that you may prosper in everything you do. 10 All of you are standing today in the presence of the Lord your God—your leaders and chief men, your elders and officials, and all the other men of Israel, 11 together with your children and your wives, and the foreigners living in your camps who chop your wood and carry your water. 12 You are standing here in order to enter into a covenant with the Lord your God, a covenant the Lord is making with you this day and sealing with an oath, 13 to confirm you this day as his people, that he may be your God as he promised you and as he swore to your fathers, Abraham, Isaac and Jacob. 14 I am making this cov-

enant, with its oath, not only with you 15 who are standing here with us today in the presence of the Lord our God but also with those who are not here today.

16 You yourselves know how we lived in Egypt and how we passed through the countries on the way here. 17 You saw among them their detestable images and idols of wood and stone, of silver and gold. 18 Make sure there is no man or woman, clan or tribe among you today whose heart turns away from the Lord our God to go and worship the gods of those nations; make sure there is no root among you that produces such bitter poison.

19 When such a person hears the words of this oath and they invoke a blessing on themselves, thinking, "I will be safe, even though I persist in going my own way," they will bring disaster on the watered land as well as the dry. 20 The Lord will never be willing to forgive them; his wrath and zeal will burn against them. All the curses written in this book will fall on them, and the Lord will blot out their names from under heaven. 21 The Lord will single them out from all the tribes of Israel for disaster, according to all the curses of the covenant written in this Book of the Law.

22 Your children who follow you in later generations and foreigners who come from distant lands will see the calamities that have fallen on the land and the diseases with which the Lord has afflicted it. 23 The whole land will be a burning waste of salt and sulfur—nothing planted, nothing sprouting, no vegetation growing on it. It will be like the destruction of Sodom and Gomorrah, Admah and Zeboyim, which the Lord overthrew in fierce anger. 24 All the nations will ask: "Why has the Lord done this to this land? Why this fierce, burning anger?"

25 And the answer will be: "It is because this people abandoned the covenant of the Lord, the God of their ancestors, the covenant he made with them when he brought them out

of Egypt. 26 They went off and worshiped other gods and bowed down to them, gods they did not know, gods he had not given them. 27 Therefore the Lord's anger burned against this land, so that he brought on it all the curses written in this book. 28 In furious anger and in great wrath the Lord uprooted them from their land and thrust them into another land, as it is now."

29 The secret things belong to the Lord our God, but the things revealed belong to us and to our children forever, that we may follow all the words of this law.

All these blessings shall overcome thee and overtake thee.

"So then faith comes by hearing, and hearing by the word of God." (Romans 10:17, NKJV)

Connect enough so that you can hear it; stay connected by reading the Word, praying and attending church.

God will do the same for everybody. He will give us an abundant life.

"The thief's purpose is to steal and kill and destroy. My purpose is to give them a rich and satisfying life." (John 10:10 NLT)

Jesus' name gives you authority.

It's not God if it's killing me, stealing from me or destroying my life; (poverty) cannot be from God.

"Whatever is good and perfect is a gift coming down to us from God our Father, who created all the lights in the heavens. He never changes or casts or casts a shifting shadow." (James 1:17 NLT)

Your life is at stake. The wages of sin are death.

But God!

Says I come to give you life – He gave us life/redeems our life- paid for what we did.

"And thou shalt speak unto the children of Israel, saying, If a man die, and have no son, then ye shall cause his inheritance to pass unto his daughter. And if he have no daughter,

then ye shall give his inheritance unto his brethren. And if he have no brethren, then ye shall give his inheritance unto his father's brethren. And if his father have no brethren, then ye shall give his inheritance unto his kinsman that is next to him of his family, and he shall possess it: and it shall be unto the children of Israel a statute of judgment, as the Lord commanded Moses. And the Lord said unto Moses, Get thee up into this mount Abarim, and see the land which I have given unto the children of Israel. And when thou hast seen it, thou also shalt be gathered unto thy people, as Aaron thy brother was gathered." (Numbers
The power of God manifests in us (Dunamis Power). We have protection as a Christian; no spells or poison can hurt us.
A Christian is someone who has a relationship with Jesus.
Jesus is the only way to heaven. "Jesus saith unto him, I am the way, the truth, and the life: no man cometh unto the Father, but by me." (John 14:6 KJV)

Know God's plan and the devil's plan (by discernment or by hearing His voice).

"Be sober, be vigilant; because your adversary the devil walks about like a roaring lion, seeking whom he may devour' (I Peter 5:8 NKJV).
Confusion and envy are from the enemy.
Is the devil stealing your time?
Light makes darkness flee. "Arise, shine; for your light has come! And the glory of the Lord is risen upon you. For behold, the darkness shall cover the earth, And deep darkness the people; But the Lord will arise upon you, And His glory shall be seen upon you. The Gentiles shall come to your light, And kings to the brightness of your rising. Lift up your eyes all around, and see: they all gather together, they come to you; Your sons shall come from afar, And your daughters shall be

nursed at your side. Then you shalt see and become radiant, And your heart shall swell with joy; Because the abundance of the sea shall be turned to you, the wealth of the Gentiles shall come to you." (Isaiah

"Submit yourselves therefore to God. Resist the devil, and he will flee from you." (James 4:7 KJV)

You don't have to fight hard; just show a little resistance and he will flee. We are the strong ones. The devil can't do anything to us. Just put up a little resistance.

"Lest Satan should get an advantage of us: for we are not ignorant of his devices" (2 Corinthians 2:11 KJV).

We have to win the battle NOW! Reach destiny, our NOW! Things or situations being deferred does make the heart sick (when we get disappointed in life). He (God) will speak, and He does everything decently and in order; He will tell you what to do first. The Holy Spirit will not condemn you but will convict you. You might cry for a second (don't stay there - the devil will beat you up and condemn you) but get in FAITH quickly!

The more you focus on yourself the more distracted you will be. The more you commune with Him the more you will be like HIM, have understanding, and be satisfied in your own heart (real satisfaction, not just for a moment).

Be not only a hearer of the word but a doer and be blessed- don't let the next thing distract you. Don't let the noise of the world keep you from hearing the voice of the Lord. "But if you look carefully into the perfect law that sets you free, and if you do what it says and don't forget what you heard, then God will bless you for doing it" (James 1:25 NLT). Nothing is more important than His presence.

"Whosoever catches a glimpse of the revealed counsel of God-the free life! - even out of the corner of his eye, and sticks with it, is no distracted scatterbrain but a man or woman of action, That person will find delight and affirmation in

the action" (James 1:25 MSG).
We are of God; not a scattered human but a holy, wise being full of love, hope and joy!
Matthew 14:28-29 (NLT) "Then Peter calls to him, 'Lord if it's really you, tell me to come to you, walking on the water.' 'Yes, come,' Jesus said. So Peter went over the side of the boat and walked on the water toward Jesus."
(Then he got distracted-looking at wrong thing)
"But when he saw the wind and waves, he was terrified and began to sink" (Matthew 14:30, NLT).
Don't look at stuff around you; keep your eyes on Jesus. Don't get distracted and then entangled. Come out of whatever struggle you are in; don't stay in the mud, grab God's hand.
No more delays to our promised land. Focus. Get to the house of God. Seek His face in your own house.
Trust.
What God says is first, is first.
Pray: Lord, we need Yyou! Jesus, help.
***If you are not going; I'm not going*** John 13:36b NKJV, "Jesus answered him, 'Where I am going you cannot follow Me now, but you shall follow Me afterward.'" John 14:3-4 NKJV says "And if I go and prepare a place for you, I will come again and receive to myself; that where I am, there you maybe also. And where I go you know, and the way you know."

We are the solution.
We have weapons of warfare!
We pray up and down the road.
We are designed to fix the problem!
We are the light.
Daniel 10:1 (NLT), "In the third year of the reign of King Cyrus of Persia, Daniel (also known as Belteshazzar) had another vision. He understood that the vision concerned events

certain to happen in the future- times of war and great hardship."

Things are getting better and better in the overall big picture of life. Sometimes I feel stuck in a never-ending doomed cycle, like Groundhogs Day, but I can see that things are getting better. God is greater than the ups and downs of life. I will not believe the lies of the enemy that say "Doom is just repetitive no matter what I do." I know that there are still some struggles in my life, although I see good happening and I know that God will sustain me. I will stay positive knowing, therefore having hope, waiting for God. He will clear the rest of the wreckage from my past escapades of rebellion while drinking and smoking, not prioritizing my kids or being faithful in attending church to hear the Word of God or read it as I should have been.

I know that I will come out with my nursing license unencumbered because the Lord told me that I would be a Nurse Practitioner. I have increased financially, and I am joyful alone. Although I am never alone. (During editing, I can see how far I've come. Once constantly overcome by sadness, desiring and believing that I needed a husband, to being joyful knowing that I am happy and can depend solely on God. He is Jehovah Jireh and provides provide for me and my children. I don't have to have the "traditional" family unit to be whole and I can raise my kids to serve God and have good lives. We don't have to care what others think; we can just enjoy life every day, live and be blessed.

He gives us wisdom to see and hear His will. Sometimes I get off track and forget but I'm always led back quickly as He will not forsake us. I can decide without having to get others' approval. Sometimes His direction is from another or a sign, but He also gives direct thoughts that we know are from Him. However, there are times I want confirmation of what I have thought due to self-doubt. Either way, if I don't sin directly or go against His will directly, everything comes out better more quickly. Solutions happen. I am prettier, happier, wiser, more prosperous, a better mom and community member. I have been more focused on my kids and their lives than ever before. I provide for them and am there for them instead of just chasing my tail to provide, remaining broke and neglecting them. Tithing and not chasing money leads to a peaceful more abundant life!

He transferred authority to us.
"You gave them charge of everything you have made, putting all things under their authority" (Psalm 8:6 NLT).
God has crowned us with glory and honor! All things are under our feet!
We just kept going, moving forward.
We went through hell.
Born again by the word of God.
Designed to have desire for something and to have all our desires met.
We are made for signs and wonders.
Born from a woman to rule and reign when I became a new creature in Christ.
We have been recreated- God's glory is on us. New blood runs through my veins and the light in my eyes scares the enemy.

We live by every word that comes from the mouth of God.
Speak against words, not people.
I declare that I win!!!
I get back seven-fold of what was going to be taken from me - in Jesus' name.

"Jesus answered, 'It is written: 'Man shall not live on bread alone, but on every word that comes from the mouth of

God.'" (Matthew

It happens right now!!! Go out and act like the church. Be the church.

See things differently, like the whole world is blessed.
It's time for change!
We are sick of sick people!
Live your purpose.
Everything is prospering in my house!
My children are acting right!
My house is on fire for God.
Everything I touch prospers and succeeds.

I HAVE JESUS.
No doubting, no self-pity, no worrying.
JESUS has ME, my family, my friends, and my community.

My yard is pretty.
My car is beautiful.
My house is gorgeous.
We have the best clothes. People want to serve Jesus because they see us and want to be blessed too.
It's all from Jesus and His mighty blessings, favor, mercy, and grace.
We serve the Most High God! Thank You, Lord, for loving us and being with us always.

He will take a wreck and make a whole kingdom out of it. It will be better than it was before.

Do not get mad when you are going through a valley, even if it seems like hell. Know, trust, and believe that better is coming. There is an oasis, we are even okay in hell. Remember

Shadrach, Meshach, and Abed-nego in the fire. God is always with us. He will never leave us or forsake us.
NO COMPLAINING- things change in the twinkle of an eye. Suddenly Jesus will appear.

We are representatives of heaven on earth. So, everybody gets blessed.

Receive the Holy Ghost, go tarry, go wait awhile; 40 days He taught in the Kingdom on earth. Bring heaven, the Kingdom, down to earth. Before He died, He said to prepare a place. When He came back, He said make sure we have days of heaven on earth. We have KINGDOM RIGHTS as Christians.

"So that as long as the sky remains above the earth, you and your children may flourish in the land the Lord swore to give your ancestors (Deuteronomy 11:21 NLT)
We will live days of heaven on earth.
We are now the victor and not the victim.

Psalm 138:1 (NLT) "I give you thanks, O Lord, with all my heart; I will sing your praises before the gods."

We overcome the devil with the Word of God.
Don't doubt, don't give in to sin because of bad things happening. It's just lows, tests, trials, or the devil/demonic things trying to push you around.
Confess your sins; ask forgiveness and they are blotted out.

"I-yes, I alone- will blot out your sins for my own sake and will never think of them again. Let us review the situation together, and you can present your case to prove your innocence" (Isaiah 43:25 NLT).

Everything is permissible but not everything is beneficial.
1 Corinthians 10:23 (NLT), "You say, 'I am allowed to do anything,' but not everything is good for you. You say, 'I am allowed to do anything,' but not everything is beneficial."
God wants to bless, love, and spend time with us. He blots our sins out for Himself. Therefore, we trust God.
Pray/Speak: Heal my land (life); forgive my sin.
Jesus must give up His spirit.
We are victors.
We are not ashamed.

We receive it!
Specific plans: listen to God to win the victory.
Do whatever the Holy Ghost tells you to do.
Leaders follow the leader (The Holy Spirit).

"Let us discern for ourselves what is right: let us learn together what is good" (Job 34:4 NIV).
We are the light of Christ.
Kingdom of God, living heaven on earth, being humble and excellent in everything that we do. Romans 16:19b (NLT) "Be wise in doing right and to stay innocent of any wrong."

## MANIFEST MIRACLES NOW

"I will bless those who bless you and curse those who treat you with contempt. All the families on earth will be blessed through you" (Genesis 12:3, NLT).
"'Bring all the tithes into the storehouse so there will be enough food in my Temple. If you do,' says the Lord of Heaven's Armies, 'I will open the windows of heaven for you. I will pour out a blessing so great you won't have enough room to take it in! Try it! Put me to the test!'" (Malachi 3:10 NLT)

Laughter is good medicine.
We need to repent (ask forgiveness) and "This do in remembrance of ME" partake of the Lord's supper often. If you can, try to do it daily to refresh yourself spiritually and physically by remembering His body and blood bore our sins on the cross to make us whole: spirit, soul and body. This takes away physical ailments, causes soundness of mind, and restores youth. We should eat healthily (fruits, vegetables, lean meats and water). We should exercise, even if only walking 30 minutes a day five days a week.

# Chapter Six
# The Beatitudes

Jesus said,
"Blessed are the poor in spirit, for theirs is the kingdom of heaven.
Blessed are those who mourn, for they will be comforted.
Blessed are the meek, for they will inherit the earth.
Blessed are those who hunger and thirst for righteousness, for they will be filled.
Blessed are the merciful, for they will be shown mercy.
Blessed are the pure in heart, for they will see God.
Blessed are those who are persecuted because of righteousness, for theirs is the kingdom of heaven.
Blessed are you when people insult you, persecute you and falsely say all kinds of evil against you because of me. Rejoice and be glad because great is your reward in heaven, for in the same way they persecuted the prophets who were before you."
(Matthew 5:3-12 NIV)

## The Fruits of the Spirit

Galatians 5: 22-23

Love
Joy
Peace
Forbearance
Kindness
Goodness
Faithfulness
Gentleness
Self-control

# Books I Read

That Helped Me Progress on my Journey:

Battlefield of the mind, Confident Woman and a little declaration book by Loyce Meyer
Not to mention daily devotional books
The Purpose Driven Life by Rick Warren
Life Ready Woman, Shaunti Feldhahn
Life Interrupted, Priscilla Shirer
Get Out of That Pit, Beth Moore
The One Year Bible, which I read four times after starting out reading Psalms and Proverbs daily- one chapter of Proverbs per day like chapter one on the 1st. Read Proverbs to distinguish foolishness from wisdom. It is also best to read first thing in the morning. Not only do you start your day out right but there is a law of first that this works with propelling your life forward -same as tithing – "first fruits".

# Acknowledgements

Pastors who have influenced my life and this book:
James Holt, Timothy Magee, Delmar Coward, Mr. and Mrs. Earl Faust, Tiffany Blackwell,
The Osteens, John Gray, Tauren Wells, Kanye West, Joyce Meyer, Perry Stone, Steven Furtick, Mike Todd, Louie Giglio, and TD Jakes.

Be ye transformed.
Pray, Praise, Read and declare word and spend time in His presence (relationship).
Can't look back- We are not going that way! Our past is not worth losing our future!
With all of this and the deep look into my life, heart and even my thoughts, I can't wait to publish this, despite my life still not being where it is going to be, so everyone can know that they are not alone on this journey. We all have difficulties and even some every day, but we can and will be able to live joyously as long as we keep our eyes on Jesus and not on our current circumstances. If you have any question as to whether or not you are saved, then examine your heart. The Word says, "that if you confess with your mouth the Lord Jesus and believe in your heart that God has raised Him from the dead, you will be saved (Romans 10:9-10 NKJV). So, there you go, no more doubting, no more fear!
Oh, and if you are ever in fear and don't know what to do or pray, just say the name of Jesus over and over and you will be delivered. Also, remember to pray in tongues that the utterance of spirit to spirit might edify you. This is not selfishness, as we must be emotionally, spiritually, and physically healthy to help, edify and encourage others. We will survive

no matter what; they can't stop us. Live a life thriving in Jesus and just keep pushing toward your dreams. Don't give up. Don't allow them to call you a quitter because you can't quit anyway! Might as well enjoy this life!!! As my mom used to always declare: "This is the day the Lord has made; We will rejoice and be glad in it" (Psalm 118:24 NKJV).

I am still believing for my house/property/inheritance/husband. John Hagee said, "We only have one spouse, not a team of connections."

# Journal

(my life continued after the start of writing)

Praise God, I overcame bulimia!10/1/2019

Breaking cycles- tests or the devil trying to make believers look stupid…. Had thoughts of every week stuff just looking bad and keep going through things over and living life just to work things out. Rest in God and allow Him to work but step up and obey when told something to do. But also have to step up and say No. Do not open the door to the devil second to lack of wisdom but do all of Christ's demands and then stand. He will send people to help you and keep you moving forward. Key words spoken over days or several days that correspond in relation to moving forward in journey.

Last week (Friday) the college told me that I couldn't do clinicals with an encumbered license. I had just signed a reprimand order settlement with the nursing license board to keep from having my license suspended and being able to continue to work and support my children. I called an attorney today (Tuesday) after going for two job interviews yesterday (Monday) and not being hired. The attorney mentioned going back to TPAPN when I thought that I was being released from that, but it is better than having disciplinary action on my license and not being able to complete the Family Nurse Practitioner program for three years because of not even being able to start clinicals for two years. With an attorney I might be able to get a warning and go back to TPAPN. The warning is a year of indirect supervision but still encumbers my license as opposed to a reprimand with stipulations which is a year of direct supervision and a year of indirect supervision. I could possibly stay at my current position in Home Health with a warning.

I was very upset on Friday, learning that I couldn't do clinicals since I was told two weeks prior that I probably could and went forward with the working interview (in a severe flood that which closed many businesses in the area). Despite working nights, I went back again the next week with no sleep. I didn't drop the class. I got a 95.5 on homework that I was stressing about doing. I was offered money to pay for an attorney.

I had a declaratory order prior to obtaining my nursing license. I have a past criminal history including: arrests for public intoxication and assaults that were dismissed/not billed. I had a conviction for possession of marijuana when I was 18 and received deferred adjudication. After the declaratory order I received the two DWIs in one week.

I was proposed to on Sat 10/12/19 by a recent widower that seems very close to the Lord.

A sherriff called me today (late October) regarding Tony's car that I had parked in open view in August. He stated that the car would not be reported stolen as Tony had texted the day that I parked it in August (I had to borrow a car for a few days and then bought one.) I had to explain to the officer that I had been driving the car for over a year and made a payment in June of $400 which he stated was taken by Child Support and he didn't pay the note. In July he then asked for $740, and I asked if he was going to pay the other $400 and if he would give me login information to pay myself. In August, he then asked me to pay $1600 and stated that he would pay the $400 but that shows an increase to $1200 which is correct without him paying anything. I did not contact him after my father died as my pastor told me not to respond to him and he was only saying demeaning things.

I am still praying about and waiting on my exoneration from the BON so that I can continue practicing as a nurse and in my nurse practitioner program being able to do clinicals and my license not having any disciplinary action. I was also offered another position at a prison and received the offer letter after two months, but they are still waiting on clearance from the Texas Department of Criminal Justice. I have not come to understand God's timing in things. All I can do is trust the process and let God fight my battles knowing that He will get all the glory. I sometimes think how my life can be an example to others if my life does not seem enjoyable or fulfilling but God gets the glory even in the turmoil and shows that we can be strong and enjoy life even when going through things and not being certain of my future because I am certain that He will never let me go or forsake me. I was able to enjoy my son's 6th birthday a couple of weeks ago at a trampoline park and my daughter had her 10th this past weekend with a sleepover, church, out to eat and to a movie. I am still working nights at a pediatric home health agency providing care for an amazing 3-year-old boy with Vein of Galen malformation which is a vascular disorder. He has had five brain surgeries, strokes, and is nourished by a G-J tube (Gastrostomy-jejunostomy tube; it's placed in the stomach and small intestine).

. He currently has seizures frequently and the family is constantly taking him to doctors appointments and therapy appointments. My heart longs for a miracle in this family's life. He is such a kindhearted little boy with siblings and parents that love him and struggle to give him the best life possible. I hope that they are able to overcome their circumstances and for complete healing for all of them physically and emotionally. While I hate not being with my own kids, it is an honor and a blessing to be able to serve this wonderful family and hopefully bring God's light and love into their home and their future. While I might not be ministering in third world countries, I feel that I am doing my part here. They are planning a trip to a neurologist in New York to hopefully stop the

seizing. I am finishing my last class (with the exception of one make-up class) prior to clinicals in my NP program and waiting to hear from the prison. I believe that God's plan will all align accordingly, even my marriage or not to this man. Is he a con or the man that I have been praying for?
How do things seem backwards, like accountability and being monitored, yet living a life holier than others? So many people these days say that obeying the law is legalism, yet Proverbs 28:4 NLT says, "To reject the law is to praise the wicked; to obey the law is to fight them." (Here is an example of Spiritual warfare). Threatened to be placed on "bad nurse" list for trying to help. BUT GOD. They even gave me a book to not "people please" but understand why others don't do things to move life forward. We are to help others; do not worry about yourself. We must listen to the Spirit's leading day by day, moment by moment.
Colossians 3:23 NLT "Work willingly at whatever you do, as though you were working for the Lord rather than for people." Proverbs 28:18 NLT "The blameless will be rescued from harm, but the crooked will be suddenly destroyed."
Judge Everything by the Word.
You can't allow what you are going through to keep you from what you are going to. Don't let the world take your property. Fight! I've been through a lot of stuff, and I could let that get me down if I dwell on it, but the truth is that carried me through it all. It wasn't me, it was Him.
If you make me fight, I'm going to win because the Lord fights my battles. He surrounds me as with a shield. All I need to do is rest and continue to follow His guidance. I believe and I speak that God is on my side, and He will not allow me to be oppressed any longer. I declare freedom from bondage to serving others and not obtaining what is rightfully mine. God wants us to serve but He also wants us blessed and not in wanting while others flourish. He is rescuing me from pov-

Milton Keynes UK
Ingram Content Group UK Ltd.
UKHW050434280324
440101UK00016B/1084